Canon
EOS
600

EOS 630 in U.S.A.
and Canada

Günter Spitzing

HOVE~FOUNTAIN BOOKS

In the USA and Canada
the Canon EOS 600 is known as the
Canon EOS 630
All text, illustrations and data apply to cameras with either name
US Edition ISBN 0-906447-59-3

Canon EOS 600
First English Edition January 1990
English Translation: Liselotte Sperl
Translation Editor: Georgina Fuller
Technical Editor: George Wakefield
Sub-editing & Design: Shirley Kilpatrick
Typeset by Icon Publications Limited, Kelso, Scotland
Printed in Germany by Kösel GmbH, Kempten

ISBN 0-86343-240-9

Published by
HOVE FOUNTAIN BOOKS
the joint imprint of

Fountain Press Ltd	&	Hove Foto Books
45 The Broadway, Tolworth		34 Church Road, Hove
Surrey KT6 7DW		Sussex BN3 2GJ

UK Trade Distribution by
Fountain Press Ltd

Contents

Data to keep you informed – audible and visual
Camera-shake warning signal – autofocus confirmation signal – important information displayed in the viewfinder – the LCD panel: three types of information.
Focusing – AF (automatic) or M (manual)
Manual focusing – fully automatic focusing – the elusiveness of sharpness – one-shot focusing or focus-lock – the AF mode baffled – what now?
Exposure by automatic program mode
No possibility of over-exposure – centre-weighted metering lock.
Creative over-ride facilities in exposure metering
Small bright subjects in front of dark backgrounds – small dark details in front of a bright background – partial metering – exposure lock independent of focusing – zoom metering – exposure over-ride.
Fully automatic flash – the intelligent automatic
Through the lens exposure control with system flashgun – infrared distance metering in complete darkness – when to use exposure compensation – LCD panel illumination.
Programmed image control
Seven preset modes – P 1 standard program mode – P 2 snapshot program – P 3 landscape program – P 4 sports program – P 5 portrait program – P 6 close-up program – P 7 interiors program.

PART IV   Programs of the EOS 600   106

Setting the Main switch – *((.)) or A*
Automatic program mode with special functions
Shifting the exposure/shutter speed values – exposure compensation or over-ride – partial metering – program shift with exposure compensation.
Av – aperture priority mode
You set the aperture, the shutter speed is calculated automatically. Av programming – changing the aperture setting – Av partial metering with shift facility – Flash in Av mode.
Tv – shutter priority mode
You choose the shutter speed – the camera determines the aperture. Tv mode functions – changing pre-selected shutter speed – Tv partial metering – flash in Tv mode.
Manual setting of aperture and shutter speed
Manual program, useful in a variety of situations – using manual mode – metering for correct exposure in Manual mode – M partial metering – Long exposures of any duration – flash in M program – the creative flash mode.
Depth of field
Previewing the depth of field by button – the depth of field mode.

Foreword

Hello 600 – Welcome into the EOS Family

The EOS camera system is one that offers the greatest range of programming facilities without the need for accessories. This book has been written in the hope of familiarizing you with all the facilities offered by the EOS 600 so that you may make full use of this wonderful camera.

Even though it is most unlikely that you will understand initially all the subtleties and the tricks possible with the EOS 600, I have made it my task to help you use your new camera from the very first moment you take it into your hand. Part III of this book should help you learn quickly all the automatic functions, so that you can take pin-sharp and perfectly-exposed pictures right from the start. Once you have mastered this aspect, you can explore the other programs and facilities for dealing with special problems and situations.

The Decisive Factor – The EOS Idea

No camera can be better than its underlying principle. The EOS idea is a logical result arising from the recognition that – and this includes both mechanical and electronically-controlled systems – in one respect at least, the limits of technical development have been reached; for every exposure program and additional function that a camera offers, it has to be fitted with an additional operating element – a slider switch, a button, a wheel or knob. This left the designers with one of two possibilities; either the camera would be so over-laden with buttons and their appropriate legends, in the shape of symbols and words, that it could be impossible to find one's way through the maze of facilities; or the number of functions would have to be reduced to render the arrangement manageable.

The problem was to produce a camera with a large range of functions that was still easy to use. This required a totally new concept in camera construction. The Canon engineers had to look around and refer to another branch of technology which had a long tradition in accommodating and managing a great variety of functions, which was computer technology.

Do not misunderstand me, though; the EOS is no computer and there never was any intention of dressing an EOS camera up as one. However,

A path disappearing into the distance with a shrub in the foreground. Automatic focusing on the blooms at the centre of the frame.

the operating elements of the EOS cameras have been arranged according to principles used in computers. The preconditions and choices – described these days as "options" – may not exactly offer unlimited possibilities but they offer much more than can be presented by individual elements. The choice of options is performed by following two or sometimes three steps; the broad field of options is sub-divided into several groups of functions – generally referred to as "menus" – and these can be recalled by operating one or several elements (i.e. displaying the function and simultaneously presenting it for choice). A further step is the activation of the required function.

Exposure compensation setting requires two steps: 1) press the exposure compensation button **EXP. COMP,** activating the facility for entering a value for over- or underexposure with simultaneous display in the LCD panel. 2) turn the input dial in either direction to set the degree of exposure compensation up to ±5 stops.

The EOS cameras have only three types of operating elements;
• The main switch, to the left of the viewfinder
• The operating buttons, arranged in various locations on the body
• The electronic input dial, on the right-hand shoulder of the camera.

1. The main switch: serves as main on/off switch and also as selector switch for one or two basically very different operating modes.

The main on/off switch is a selector switch. The green rectangle is the setting for fully automatic program mode.

i) Uncomplicated automatic operation: turn main switch counter-clockwise with the green rectangular symbol on top. In this setting the camera is switched on and works in fully automatic mode. Almost all special functions are de-activated. Most operating elements will not respond.

ii) Operation with a variety of creative functions: turn main switch clockwise with either symbol **A** or **((.))** on top. All operating elements are switched on.

Function buttons behind the switch cover at the rear of the camera.

2. Operating elements: some of the 10 buttons activate special functions. However, most of them will select a function and simultaneously activate the input dial to enter that function which is then displayed in the LCD panel.

3. The electronic input dial: this is used to select a function or value from the functions or values displayed in the LCD panel and previously selected by one of the operating elements. This could be an exposure program or a value, such as an exposure compensation.

The electronic input dial. This is used to select a particular program – after pressing the appropriate button first – or it selects the value of a particular preselected function. So, for example, one can select exposure compensations between –0.5 and –5.0 and +0.5 and +5.0 f-stops.

This is the EOS idea – the solution to the problem of offering a wide variety of functions within a camera whilst retaining easy operation by this three-step choice of options.

Practical Tips Versus Photographic Theory

My main concern has been to keep this book clear and simple in its layout. When you start exploring some complex photographic situation you may want to check up on a certain point. After all, the necessity of exposure bracketing does not arise every day. To help you find the appropriate reference quickly I shall have to repeat myself at times. You will, for example, find references to flash photography under aperture priority mode (Program Av), under shutter speed priority mode (Program Tv), and also under EOS flash photography.

Dummy Runs – First Without a Film

To be able to use your EOS 600 you will need a lithium battery (type 2CR5). When buying the camera it will generally be supplied with a battery. Release the screw at the right side of the camera body with a coin and remove the handgrip. This opens up the battery compartment immediately above the camera base. Insert the battery with both contacts pointing inwards and its convex side pointing towards the camera base.

Now you can release the shutter to take the first picture. First you should practise the operation of the release button, as this has several functions and is a very important operation.

One thing I would like to recommend that you do at once is to buy a spare battery. Although this special battery is sufficient to keep you in power for a fair number of films, I know from my own experience that the first battery may be exhausted sooner then you think. A new toy needs to be played with and every time you lightly press the release activating the focusing and exposure metering systems, every time the audible alarm sounds, battery power is used. I should not worry too much about what seems excessive power consumption. When you are familiar with the camera, the battery will last much longer.

The First Film for your EOS 600

To start with I recommend that you use a fast film, say ISO 400 slide film. This ensures complete success even for the very first series of pictures and success from the very beginning will encourage you to further pursue your photography with the EOS 600. I recommended that you use a slide film as this will give you a clear indication of whether you will want to rely on the automatic film speed setting of your EOS 600 or

"Good morning to all of you"
Shot in natural interior light with a fast film (exposed at ISO 800/30°)

whether you might prefer to override the automatic film speed setting when exposing a film for a particular requirement. With regard to the topic of correctly exposed pictures I would like to say that this is to some extent a matter of taste and only you can decide whether you want slightly denser or less dense pictures. One also has to consider that although one make and model of camera may look exactly the same as another, because of some mechanical imprecision, or tolerances, they may vary slightly from each other. For this reason it is important to find out whether your camera tends towards slight over- or underexposure and whether this corresponds exactly to your personal taste. I have tested four EOS cameras and found that they all tended towards slight overexposure to the same extent. This is quite convenient for colour and black-and-white print films as they are better given slightly generous exposures. It is not so satisfactory for slide film as this should never be overexposed.

However, the first time you take pictures with your EOS do not apply any compensations, just allow the camera's exposure metering system to take control.

Only two further measures have to be taken before you can begin.

• Turn the main switch clockwise until the green rectangle is showing and **P**, for program mode, is displayed in the LCD panel.

The rectangle at the centre of the viewfinder, indicated by the two brackets, is the AF target field. The AF mechanism focuses on the subject detail within the rectangle.

- Check that the slide switch on the lens is set to **AF**, for autofocus, otherwise the autofocus function will not work. Now you can start your first photographic session! You need only to press the shutter release button, which has several functions.

- Firstly, there is the possibility of pressing the release button fully down. The autofocus function of your EOS will immediately spring into action and focus on the subject detail within the target field, an audible tone will indicate that it has found a satisfactory focus, and the shutter will operate to make the exposure. The whole process takes just a fraction of a second. In the time it takes to read this paragraph, you could have taken a dozen pictures.

- The second possibility is a light pressure on the release. Your right forefinger can detect the first pressure point quite easily, half-way down the full path. In this position the release button will just be level with the surface of the indent in which it is set, and your finger can rest there quite comfortably.

1. The focusing process is started.

2. Both focus and exposure settings are stored as long as you keep your finger on the button. If you do not want to use this setting, take your finger off the release button and restart the procedure.

3. Both the focus setting and exposure setting are stored as long as the release button is pressed half-way. In order to restart a metering sequence, the release button has to be released and pressed again.

The latter process is always important when you wish to keep control of the focusing and framing of the subject. Let's assume that you wish to take a photograph of a tree that has to be sharply focused with the surrounding areas being unsharp, but the tree is supposed to be placed off-centre towards the edge of the frame. You proceed as follows:

- Focus on the tree by placing it within the AF target field.
- Lightly press the release. The AF mechanism will focus sharply on the tree detail within the AF target field.
- Keep the release pressed and swing the camera to the left, placing the tree towards the right edge of the frame.
- Fully press the release button.

This is a typical snapshot subject. This most important detail that has to be in sharp focus lies exactly in the centre of the frame. For this type of shot press your finger down fully on the release, correct focus is indicated by an audible tone (AF ready signal). All this is accomplished in a fraction of a second providing the subject is bright enough.

Of Snapshot Photographers and Careful Arrangers

Most owners of an EOS camera are very happy with their choice, but we all use our camera differently. Generally we can distinguish snapshot photographers from those who think and plan. The snapshot photographer tends to take the majority of his pictures with a "lead" index finger – he sees a suitable subject, points the camera, and down comes his index finger. This is fair enough and usually quite successful. Most subjects of this type will lie at the centre of the frame, or be at a certain distance so that the whole subject is uniformly sharp across the whole frame. The AF function and exposure mode of the EOS will do the rest to ensure perfectly focused and exposed pictures. Photographers in this category tend to have a preference for symmetry and balance; they tend to be self-assured and of quick reaction. For them, photography is a means of bringing some order into our world of confusing detail and contradictory information.

This is a typical focus/re-align/release subject. The important figures in the composition (the two boys) fill the right and the left side of the picture. The part of the picture where the AF frame falls consists of totally unstructured and unimportant background. In such a situation, if you try to press the release down fully the AF mechanism will traverse the full focusing range from close-up to infinity, as there is no structure within the target field on which it can focus, and then it will give up. To obtain a satisfactory result, a suitable point has to be placed within the AF target field, say the eyes of one of the boys, then, keeping the release pressed, re-align the camera for the desired framing and the release can now be fully pressed to make the exposure.

Then there are others – and I count myself amongst them – who are more adventurous, photographers who tend to try out several angles and aspects before finally pressing the release. Photographers like these tend to check the picture they wish to create by careful inspection in the viewfinder. Those of us who work in this way may be described as seekers, who wish to see and reveal what may be hidden behind the obvious. We hope to be able to take pictures that reveal underlying meanings and depths but we also ask ourselves repeatedly whether we could not have improved on what we did. Naturally, there will hardly be anybody who uses his EOS exclusively in one way or the other. The way I use my camera depends to a large extent on the subject. After all, if I wish to catch a cyclist, I cannot hesitate long; on the other hand, a close-up of a beautiful flower will take some attention for proper focusing and carefully arranged depth of field to show it to the best advantage.

I don't know how experienced you are in taking pictures.

In case you think you are a novice, then start by reading Part II where you will find a description of how to get your camera ready to take pictures and then go on to Part III, which has been written to help you use the EOS with ease. Just a few hours studying these pages and you can start. For an explanation of how a picture is created and what possibilities there are at your disposal for the creation of a picture as you may see it in your mind's eye read Part I.

If you are already experienced in photography, study Part I and perhaps some of Part III which deals with the practical aspects of handling the camera.

Even if you already own an EOS camera but not the EOS 600 then you will find Part III very instructive as this latest EOS model introduces many new features.

Part I

Learn About Photography – Take Better Pictures

The Characteristics of the Photographic Image

If you want to take good pictures, keep seven things in mind!

Photographs are a very specific type of visual representation. They possess seven typically photographic characteristics. By necessity these result to a large extent from the conditions of photographic technique and practical situations – conditions which define the limits within which our creative urge can be expressed. Each photograph:

- is exposed more or less correctly. It may look a little dark or a little light;
- possesses a certain contrast between the light and the dark areas. The contrast can be large or small and depends, among other factors, on the subject;
- is sharp – partly or across the whole frame – at least, it is supposed to be!
- possesses a certain reproduction scale;
- is restricted to, by necessity, a certain section taken from the subject space;
- has a rectangular frame;
- is influenced by the colouring of the subject. This is rendered either in colour or in grey tones, whose values depend on the luminosity of the colours.

These seven characteristics of the photographic process could be considered the basics that our camera, together with the photographic materials, puts in our hands as a creative tool.

Topic 1: Image Creation through Exposure

Perhaps you will think it a bit peculiar if I talk of image creation together with exposure. After all, the opinion that there are an uncountable number of incorrect exposures for one situation but only one correct one, is widely held.

The correct Exposure depends on:

- *The intensity of the illumination*
- *The reflectance of the subject*
- *The speed of the film used – low speed film, for example an ISO 25/15°, requires much more exposure than an ISO 400/27°.*

The choice of the correct shutter speed/aperture combination will ensure that the correct amount of light is allowed to expose the film.

exposure time	**aperture**	**amount of light required**
short	*small*	*large amount of light*
long	*wide open*	*small amount of light*

Exposure of slide film has to be right for the highlights which are still supposed to show clear detail – slight underexposure is usually better than too generous an exposure. The exposure of colour or black-and-white print film should be calculated for the darkest areas that are still to show detail – it is usually advisable to over-expose slightly. The exposure system of EOS cameras is, as far as I can ascertain, geared towards print film and the exposure control will automatically provide correctly-exposed pictures when this type of film is used.

On the East coast of the Greek Island of Pilion.
Above: a stormy sky above the plain of Volos in the evening. My aim was to expose for the lightest details – this was easily achieved by partial metering. In this case I also applied an exposure compensation (EXP.COMP) of –0.5 *f*-stop.
Below: morning on the island of Pilion. The trees served as the focusing point for this composition.
Both shots were taken on Kodachrome 200 film.

Even if we don't have any idea what constitutes correct exposure, we will still get correctly-exposed pictures – at least as long as we set the EOS to fully automatic exposure mode (green rectangle). The speed of the film is automatically programmed into the camera computer when it is loaded. The exposure mode of the EOS 600 will automatically meter and calculate the correct exposure for every frame. However, if you know something about assessing a subject you have a real chance of getting a better picture if you determine the aperture and shutter speed yourself.

A correctly-exposed picture is a picture that shows detail both in the brightest and in the darkest subject areas, i.e. even the very bright areas hold some detail and even the deepest shadows are not totally submerged in black.

As the comparison of the two exposure sequences shows, a subject with low contrast can handle considerable over- as well as underexposure. A very contrasty subject, on the other hand, tends to be quite wrong even with a minor under- or overexposure.

Therefore we can conclude that, generally, correct exposure for a contrasty subject is the most effective. But there are exceptions! Contrasty subjects in particular are the ones where an exposure correction may be an effective means to a good picture – this is the same as saying that intentional incorrect exposure can give the most impressive effect.

If we take, for example, a brightly-lit subject in the foreground – a flower, a figure or a piece of jewellery – against a dark background, then it would be quite correct to assess the exposure for the foreground and it does not matter whether the background is more or less clearly defined. Almost all backlit shots with slide film require an exposure compensation of one stop, i.e. the shutter speed has to be reduced to half the measured value, or the aperture has to be opened up by one stop. An example of this type of situation is the colour shot of the thunderstorm and the pillion rider. There are also situations where a dark figure in the shade is the important subject detail. In this case you have no choice but to over-expose for this subject part and the bright background will have to be over-exposed by necessity.

Spring in Schleswig Holstein. The focus was on the tractor in the background. This is how I proceeded:
1. Zoom lens EF 35-105mm f3.5-4.5, focal length setting at 105mm.
2. AF target field pointed at the tractor, AF function activated by lightly pressing the release button.
3. With the shutter release still pressed to store both the AF setting and the exposure, change the zoom setting and move the camera to place the tractor at the top of the frame.
4. Complete the pressure on the shutter release.
This takes much less time and is simpler in practice than the description suggests.

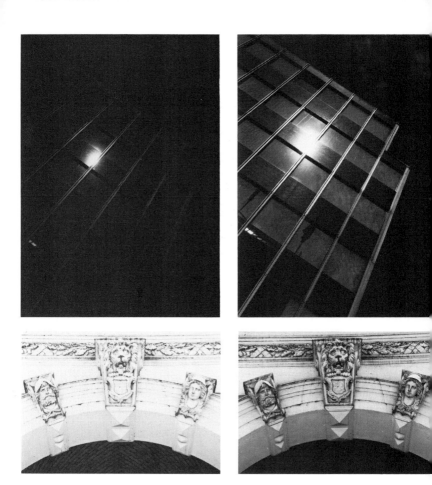

Topic 2: Image Creation through Contrast

Subject contrast plays a very important part in the effect of a picture. However, in considering contrast we have to take into account three different factors that together make up the contrast within a frame. These different factors may increase or counteract each other's effect as the case may be. In particular we are dealing with the following.

The characteristics of the film

Some types of film reproduce subject contrasts more brilliantly than others. One example of the contrasty type of film is, for example,

Three exposures of a very contrasty subject (AEB) mode:

far left: underexposure by 2 f-stops.
centre: correct exposure produced by the automatic control of the EOS 600. Both shadow and light parts show sufficient detail.
left: overexposure by two stops. The highlights are bleached.

Three exposures of a subject with low contrast (AEB) mode:

far left: overexposure by two stops, even the lightest subject areas show sufficient detail
centre: correct exposure using the automatic exposure control on the EOS 600
left: underexposure by 2 stops, even the darkest areas show sufficient detail.

Kodachrome 64. In the case of black-and-white film the contrast depends to a large extent on the processing. This topic is covered in detail in the chapter: Stage, dusk, night and interior photography without flash.

The subject contrast
The different surfaces of a subject reflect light to different degrees. Black velvet, for example, absorbs almost all the light and reflects only a small proportion. A white, crisply-starched cotton shirt, on the other

Contrast within the subject; the lightest and darkest details determine the contrast of the subject.

hand, reflects almost all the incident light. The bride dressed in white next to the groom resplendent in black, the baker in his white overalls next to a chimney sweep, a white kid next to a black lamb and even a dark red rose against the light blue sky, all these are subjects with extreme contrast ranges. Among low contrast subjects we can count two gentlemen in grey flannels against a light panelled wall, a grey parrot in a green tree, etc. Low-contrast subjects also include landscapes in the mist and even a snowscape – provided there is not a black dog in the middle of it.

Illumination contrast

Light is capable of increasing or decreasing contrast to an almost unlimited degree. Every type of illumination that throws shadows, the sun or flash and in particular side or back lighting, increases the contrast. Types of illumination that light up the shadows reduce the contrast – for example frontal illumination (e.g. flash mounted on the camera, or indirect flash pointed at the dark corners of a room). Flash illumination, in the form of indirect or fill-in flash is an excellent means of reducing subject contrast, both for backlit subjects in sunlight or subjects lit by a strong artificial light source.

This palm leaf is an example of illumination contrast. The difference between the lightest highlight and the darkest shadow defines contrast. If the illumination contrast is high it tends to overshadow the subject contrast. For low illumination contrast the subject contrast could gain the upper hand.

Silhouettes.
 The charm in such photographs lies in the sharply-defined shape of the subject. To achieve this you have to expose for the light background to render the poorly-lit silhouette subject as dark as possible.

To be an expert photographer means to be able to recognize and properly assess the subject and illumination contrasts before pressing the release. This does not mean to say that either high or low contrast range is desirable for good photography. Every subject is different and has its own particular charm and possibilities and the way you may wish to influence the illumination is a matter of practical circumstances and personal taste.

Underexposed backlit subjects, taken on slide film, count amongst the most attractive subjects. For low contrast subjects, on the other hand, one usually prefers a slow, high contrast film. For portraits it is usually desirable to fill-in heavy shadows and to produce flattering images by appropriate processing techniques and soft grades of paper in black-and-white printing.

Should you be unsure of what to do in a particular case and how to deal with the contrast, always think of the final result you wish to achieve. I assume that in the majority of cases the main subject will have to be shown in sharp focus with clear definition of all details. You therefore control the contrast to cover the important subject detail.

Example I: Subject: a horse, backlit, in front of a tree. Tree and horse produce long shadows but they are both outlined by a bright halo of light. You have to arrange your viewpoint to show the horse in clear profile against the background, making sure that the head of the horse is not superimposed on the tree trunk! You have to wait for the right moment when the outlines are clearly fringed by the light and then press the release. This is an example of where the high contrast is used to advantage to create an atmospheric image. You hope the animal does not decide exactly at the moment you press the release to turn around as the effect would be totally destroyed by the movement blur. In this case you would have to wait and hope for another opportunity.

Example II: You want to photograph the decorated wall of a farm in the Swiss Alps. The shadow of a large tree falls on the sunlit wall, obscuring the painting. If you take the picture under these conditions, the shadow of the tree will confuse the outlines and colours of the painting. The shadow has to be removed. You either have to wait until the sun moves into a different position so that the wall is either totally free of shadows or totally in the shade. Smaller subject sections could be illuminated by flash which would eliminate, or at least counteract to a large extent, the effects of the shadows.

The outline of the main subject has to be clearly defined against the background. Intersection with other objects in the fore-, middle- or background have to be avoided. Often it is sufficient to move as little as one step to the right or left, or to move closer, as in the example on this page, and the main subject presents itself clearly to the camera. Subjects with clear outlines are most attractive when the contrast is exagerated.

Topic 3: Image Creation Through Sharpness

Sharpness is, next to contrast and colour, the most important element in image creation. A picture may contain varying degrees of sharpness from total to partial. One thing it should not be is completely unsharp but here too there are exceptions.

The sharpness or unsharpness of a picture depends on several factors, namely:

- the exposure time in relation to the focal length of the lens, and
- the focus setting of the lens also in relation to the focal length

---

Exposure time: the EOS will automatically warn you of too slow shutter speeds which mean danger of camera-shake. The following rule has proved useful:
The slowest safe shutter speed = 1/lens focal length, i.e.
1/60th sec for a 50mm lens
1/125th sec for a 100mm lens
1/250th sec for a 250mm lens
In case the program mode determines a shutter speed slower than this value, an audible alarm is sounded.
Personally I like to apply more stringent limits but this is not always possible. Sometimes the lighting conditions demand slower times.
For hand-held shooting I try never to go below 1/250th sec, occasionally 1/125th sec if the light is poor. When I am using a focal length of 100mm or longer, I try to support my arm or the camera in some way.

I always try to use shutter speeds of 1/250th sec and faster for hand-held shots. As soon as I need to use slower times, I reach for a tripod or a flash. Flash illumination times are as fast as 1/1000th sec and faster.

For shutter speeds between 1/125th sec and 1/30th sec, and in case of absolute emergency even down to 1/8th sec, we could try a shot by supporting our arms on the back of a chair, a bannister, a fence, or any other sturdy object that is handy.

If the intention is to express the impact of a movement, slower shutter speeds may be used. For example, a group of cyclists racing by with their legs blurred against a sharply defined background. Such a picture will convey the speed of the cyclists much better than one taken with a fast shutter speed which would freeze any movement. To introduce movement blur of the cyclists a shutter speed of 1/30th sec or even slower will be required. Then there is the technique of using slower shutter speeds and moving the camera along with the cyclists, known as

Detail of a fishing boat in the harbour of Nea Roda, Chalkidiki with a church in the background. The different possibilities of placing the depth of field on the foreground or further into the background were tried out using the 105mm focal length setting. Smaller apertures make the unsharp objects more recognizable.

Focusing: the subject sharpness and the depth of field depend on the focal length of the lens, the subject distance and the size of the aperture.		
large aperture	*a lot of light enters the lens*	*narrow depth of field*
small aperture	*little light enters the lens*	*large depth of field*
object close to lens (e.g. flower)	*represented large in negative*	*very narrow depth of field*
object far away from lens (e.g. landscape	*represented small in negative*	*large depth of field*
long focal length lens (100mm or longer)	*large reproduction scale*	*narrow depth of field*
short focal length (50mm or shorter)	*small reproduction scale*	*very large depth of field*

panning. Now the cyclists will be relatively sharp and the background quite blurred. Naturally, this has to be done with the camera hand-held. The shutter speed can be slowed to 1/15th sec as the swift movement of following the subject counteracts any shaking of the hands.

The effect of these various techniques is quite distinct. It makes a considerable difference whether you take the rushing force of a waterfall at 1/60th or 1/1000th or even 1/2000th sec. In one case the force and speed of the water will be emphasized by the unsharp haze; in the other the movement is frozen.

The choice of sharpness within the subject space is even more important than movement blur or sharpness. The EOS 600 offers a very precise focusing mode (AF) to cope with all these situations. The following applies to sharpness, as to any other automatic function:
1. The automatic mode saves a number of manipulations.
2. The automatic mode allows a faster reaction to a given situation.

A path leading into the distance. To show everything in sharp focus, from close-up to infinity, the 35mm wide-angle setting was selected on the 35-105mm, ƒ3.5-4.5 zoom. The use of a relatively fast film – T-max ISO 400 – ensured that the program mode calculated a fast enough shutter speed together with a small aperture.

3. The automatic mode is capable of better precision than manual settings.

4. The automatic mode ensures that even hasty snapshots have a high success rate.

5. The automatic mode saves almost everything except your active decisions – particularly if the intention is carefully to arrange an image. The motto "allow yourself a few interesting hours – think a little" may be applied with good results to photography!

EOS system lenses can be focused for close-up photography without additional accessories for subject distances between 30cm and 140cm (long focal length lenses from 400cm). As a rough guide you can remember that the close-up distance in cm will more or less correspond to the focal length of the lens in mm. The greatest depth of field for any lens is always at its hyperfocal distance. A 50mm standard lens, focused at 40m, its hyperfocal distance at $f2$, will depict everything from about 20m to infinity in acceptably sharp focus, even at maximum aperture of say $f2$.

Often it is desirable to depict a path that recedes into the background or the facade of buildings down a street in absolutely sharp focus. A wide-angle lens, together with a small aperture, will ensure perfect results.

However, perfect sharpness from close-up to infinity is not always desirable. Sometimes it is more effective to separate the main subject from foreground and background by reducing the depth of field to the important message. Personally I think that pictures taken with a long lens and wide aperture are often the most impressive – the main subject in a clearly defined and sharply limited depth of field jumps out of the picture, against the blurred foreground and background. This emphasises the main message, its sharpness highlighting it against the blurred background.

With subject treatment like this, there will usually be a tendency to locate the sharpness in the foreground. However, it is not absolutely necessary; sometimes it is useful to show the background outlines relatively sharp against blurred foreground detail.

Topic 4: Image Creation Through Reproduction Scale

Have you ever thought about photography as a means of showing small objects on a large scale and large subjects on a small scale? The effect of a picture depends to a certain extent on the reproduction scale. If you show a whole castle or a view of a town district, by necessity this large subject has to be shown greatly reduced in size. When looking at the actual object we have to let our eyes wander over it to take it all in. A picture showing the same object can be assessed in an instant. The overall shape and outline of a castle, say, is easily assessed and recognized in a picture. The effects of reproduction scale are at least as staggering the other way round. If we move close to a small subject, then it appears bigger and more important in the reproduction. This applies in particular to macro photography. The effect of reproduction scales larger than actual size can be achieved even with normal lenses. Most EOS system lenses will allow a reproduction scale of 1:10, i.e. the subject is represented on film 1/10th of its original size.

Subsequent enlargement by projecting a slide or enlarging a negative, to say, 0.67cm x 1 m, results in a reproduction scale of 3:1, i.e. a linear enlargement of 3-times actual size. This lends weight to the subject or subject detail, be it a flower, coin, etc. This aspect of photography is very important as there is a special appeal in bringing far-away objects into the picture at a relatively large scale, or of showing a very small object at a large scale. From my own experience I would recommend that you go as close to the subject as possible and use longer focal lengths in most situations. This ensures that most subjects will be shown relatively large and thus gain weight, impact and importance.

Topic 5: Image Creation Through Framing

The camera could be thought of as some kind of optical scissors that cut out a clearly-defined section from the overall subject space that surrounds us. It may sound obvious to you, but I do need to repeat it here – the choice of framing does not depend on some vague idea nor should it be left to chance. It is always worthwhile to think about framing the subject correctly and to good effect; you will be rewarded with better, more effective pictures. It will not do to simply chop a subject about. Recently I came across an advertising poster with a Legong-dancer from Bali and the photographer had simply cut off her outstretched arm! This will never do! If you decide to take a portrait, think about what to include and what not. If the hands are to be shown then include both of them or they should be excluded altogether. By the way, when taking portraits of people, even if it is only their heads, it is necessary to leave a space all round, particularly in the direction of the gaze or movement.

This picture was taken at close range with the 35-105mm, ƒ3.5-4.5 zoom.

Topic 6: Image Creation Through the Rectangular Properties of the Frame

Every picture depends on the shapes and lines formed in relation to the rectangular frame. The frame is the reference system. Without the frame there could be no image composition. If there is no frame, how then would the position of the surfaces or the lines be defined? The frame is the device which limits and defines the picture. Even the decision of whether to take a picture in horizontal or vertical format can quite decisively influence the end effect.

The horizontal format emphasises the breadth and extent of land and lakes, it suits animals moving fast across the field of view, as well as motorbikes, cars and ships. The image within a horizontal format gives a normal impression. The angle of view of our eyes is also more or less a horizontal format, only it is not rectangular.

The vertical format, on the other hand, suits high subjects, mountains, trees, towers, people. It opens up like a window, revealing a view that would have stayed hidden otherwise. Upright formats give the impression of greater tension, they draw our attention strongly to the subject. The upright format expresses, more or less subtly, all the symbolism inherent in vertical lines – a tendency towards upward striving, a desire for the peaks.

Left: The horizontal format corresponds to our natural perception. It emphasizes the breadth of the landscape or the broad front of a façade. In this picture of Athos monastery Dochierchou the horizontal format emphasizes the lines of the walls and verandas.

Above: The upright format makes us see a subject in a new light. The limits of the frame are more obvious, like the view through a window or a door. The upright format emphasizes vertical lines, all lines pointing upwards to the sky and downwards towards hidden depths. In this shot of Dochiariou monastery the upright format emphasizes the height of the tower.

The most important principles are:

- keeping straight lines parallel with the sides. Any lines in the subject should be aligned to the horizontal or vertical lines of the frame.
- contrasting the lines within the subject with the frame. Important lines are arranged on a diagonal. Special emphasis is drawn to diagonal lines and objects along that diagonal.
- centering of subject areas or points of interest. A main subject – perhaps a light head against a dark background, or perhaps the other way round, a dark head against a light background – is arranged at the centre of the frame. This we tend to do quite spontaneously when we lift a camera to our eyes. The majority of photographs show the main subject at the centre of the frame. This is also the reason why the AF metering field of the EOS is at the centre of the frame and why the exposure metering is centre-weighted.
- the intentional arrangement of important areas away from the centre. An important visual statement is placed towards the upper or lower corner of the frame. Pictures like these demand our attention far more strongly; they hold more tension. However, compositions of this type need to be properly counterbalanced so they demand more thought.

The effect of framing is not only of limiting an area, it is also about creating a spatial effect. A picture is also a window – it provides a view of the world. From this point of view the framed image – not just framed by the outlines of the actual frame but perhaps a view across a landscape framed by branches, or views with mirrored images, or other types of frames like doorways, etc. can be particularly effective.

The Aphaia temple on Aighina. The wall on the left and the column on the right run more or less parallel to the sides of the frame and thus emphasize the effect. In addition the effect of "looking through" is created. The two architraves above the columns at the centre of the picture provide a suitable contrast, displaying the falling diagonal (from top left to bottom right) This shot was taken with a red filter, picking out the white columns against a dramatically dark sky.

The same subject under the same conditions. However, this shot was taken with the red filter which makes the sky much darker. I also printed the negative the other way round to show how different the effect of a subject can be when the direction of the diagonal is changed – either a rising or a falling diagonal.

The framed composition. This photograph is not only framed by the natural outline of the picture; the subject itself contains a frame, emphasizing the spatial effect.

Compare this with the picture above. It is the same subject without a frame – quite boring in comparison. Don't you agree?

41

Topic 7: Image Creation Through Colour

Colour film is favoured by 90% of photographers. Even using monochrome material, the colour content of a subject plays an important role. After all, the colours are translated into tones of grey in the black-and-white shot. The rendering of colours in monochrome can also be modified by the use of filters.

- Our world is composed of brilliant colours such as yellow, orange and red, and less insistent colours such as blue and green and then there are the quieter colours such as brown. Subjects consisting of strong colours are conspicuous. You will have to decide whether the main subject, that bears the important message, should be emphasized by a strong colour, or whether an unimportant subject may steal some of the attention by its strong colour.
- Perfect sharpness and strong colouring lend a subject great importance. Some compositions are effective because there is a certain tension between two statements. Perhaps a discreet colour subject detail is shown in sharp focus, whilst a less important subject area is in strong glowing colour but depicted slightly out of focus. I have used this method by obscuring the foreground of a sharply-depicted background landscape by a big splash of out-of-focus red blooms.
- The insistent colours such as red, yellow, orange, also described as warm colours, are typical foreground colours. They seem to jump out of a picture, attracting the viewer's attention. The cool colours, on the other hand, like blue and green, are more receding background colours.

Top: view across the harbour at Kiel.
Bottom: an angry sky in Franken.

These two pictures represent two opposites. The scene at the top was taken in the north of Germany and, although it was midday, the mood is rather cold; the scene below is bathed with warmer light which is characteristic of the southern part of Germany.

One thing is common to both pictures; the correct exposure depends upon the proper assessment of the proportion of light and dark areas. The problem of exposure, which is also a problem of effective image creation, can be solved in one of three ways; either by partial metering, or by integral metering with exposure compensation (EXP.COMP) between −1 and −1.5 f-stops, or by setting a faster film speed.

Search for a Subject – A Photographic Exploration of Time and Space

The Camera Moves Through Space

Photography is viewing space from different positions and angles.

- Lateral movements: each slight movement of the camera to the right or left changes the framing. But what is more important is to move not only the camera but your position. A change in shooting position changes the positions of the objects relative to each other, and this in turn is the secret of finding an interesting composition. In the case of distant objects, you would have to move a long way to change the aspect of the objects within the frame. It is not unusual for me to race a few kilometres in my car to be in time to show the sun at a certain angle relative to the peak of a mountain. Close objects, on the other hand, require just a few steps or even only centimetres to reveal different aspects.
- Pointing the camera upward or downward: swinging the camera upwards or downwards determines whether the ground or the sky dominates the picture. Taking a shot from a low or a high viewpoint changes the aspect as well, re-arranging the spatial relationship of objects.
- Traversing space with a zoom lens and/or assignment of focusing plane: changing the focal length on the lens means picking out a different section, a wider or narrower angle of view, from the subject space. After all, it is the sharpness of a subject that lends importance to the subject detail. For example, we are taking a picture of a clown in a circus who is just about to eat a curry sausage. If you focus on the eyes of the clown with his painted face and comical expression, then the face and the funny grin will be the main attraction. The sausage in front of the face, unsharply defined, is reduced to an unimportant prop. It is hardly noticed but it may distract our attention from the comical face if its blurred outlines cover important features. If, on the other hand, the focus is placed on the curry sausage and the face behind it is more or less blurred, then its presence simply adds a carnival mood and the sausage is the important object. With this treatment the sausage could well be used as an advertising poster for the promotion of curry sausages.

Monks live on the holy mountain of Athos. Focusing was quite simple by AF function, with one provision – the focus setting had to be stored as the main subject was not in the centre of the frame. The AF and exposure settings are stored in ONE SHOT mode. If the main switch is set to the green rectangle – program mode – then the ONE SHOT mode is selected automatically.

Late gothic Madonna in west portal of the Münster at Schwäbisch Gmünd. This sequence demonstrates how a slight change in shooting position together with a change in the focusing plane can greatly change the effect of an image.

The Camera Moves Through Time

When taking pictures you not only move through space, you also move through time – as well as finding the most suitable shooting position and angle of view, you also have to judge the right time to press the release. For fast-moving snapshot subjects – children at play, people dancing or at sport – timing is the important factor. The important point is to capture a subject at exactly the right moment when its outline and attitude express a particular relationship to its surroundings. The same also applies to still objects. In the case of portraits, for example, it is important to catch the right expression. In the case of landscapes, the right mood created by the illumination is the decisive factor.

The correct use of time and space are the fascinating aspects of photography. Time and space are closely related and cannot really be considered totally separate. Most subjects require a certain amount of moving about to determine the best possible angle as well as our full attention for the right moment, when the spatial aspect is correct, to press the release.

Focusing plane moving through space. The AF metering sought out the wooden ribs in the foreground in the top picture. In the picture below, the focusing plane was shifted to the ribs in the background.

Part II

Getting The EOS 600 Ready for Action

Energy from a Lithium Battery

Power Output of the 2CR5 Battery

The EOS 600 needs a powerful battery for its large variety of automatic functions. This energy source, the 2CR5 lithium battery, cannot be described as cheap. And what does this battery do? If I travel with my EOS 600, I take one battery for every 40 rolls of film with 36 exposures, and a spare one, just in case. In summer or in a hot climate, one battery should last for about 100 films. If you photograph in winter or go on an arctic exploration, then one battery will be able to expose only about 10 films at temperatures around − 20° C.

The power consumption of your EOS, and therefore how many films one battery is capable of exposing, is a difficult question, similar to how long is a piece of string? The answer depends on how frequently you make use of several special functions provided by the EOS 600. If you keep on playing with a long telephoto lens or a macro lens, continuously trying out various focus settings, or if you use the fast shooting sequence, then you should not be surprised if the battery shows early signs of exhaustion. One thing I can state with certainty; you will be lucky to expose more than 20 films with your first two batteries. The temptation to experiment with your new EOS 600 is too strong and this is essential to start with. After all, it is important that you become completely familiar with your EOS 600. On the other hand, this costs energy but it cannot be avoided.

It is advisable to remove the battery from the camera if it is not going to be used for some time, e.g. three weeks or more.

By the way, despite the wealth of functions offered with the EOS 600 it is very frugal in its requirements and you can expose more films than with any other comparable camera before the battery is exhausted.

Inserting or Replacing the Battery

- Loosen the screw in the handgrip with a coin and remove.
- If there is an exhausted battery in the compartment, tilt the camera with the left side upwards and simultaneously push back the red catch on the right of the battery compartment, and the battery will slide out into your hand.
- Insert a new battery. The two contacts should point inwards with the indented part pointing downward.

- Push the battery in until the red catch engages.
- Replace the handgrip and secure by tightening the screw. The EOS 600 will work only if the handgrip is properly secured.

bc Means Battery Check

The battery supplies energy every time the EOS is switched on and the basic data appears in the LCD panel. If the camera is switched off, and a film is loaded, the number of exposed frames is displayed in the panel together with the symbol for a loaded film – three bars.

However, these displays do not inform you of the actual state of the battery, i.e. how much energy is in reserve. It could be that a nearly-exhausted lithium battery has insufficient reserves to rewind an exposed film although the shutter can still be released. It is therefore a good idea to check, perhaps after every 3 or 4 films, how far from exhaustion the battery still is:

- Turn the main switch on the top left of the viewfinder prism from the lock position either to the green rectangle, to **((.))** or to **A**.
- Open switch cover at rear of camera and press the battery check button. As long as this button is pressed the display panel changes to show the letters **bc** and, as appropriate, 1, 2 or 3 bars.

LCD panel – if there is no battery in the camera, or if the battery is exhausted. The same display also appears if a fully charged battery, but no film, is loaded into the EOS and it is not switched on.

The display with a fully charged battery, the film loaded and the camera not switched on.

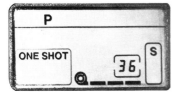

Display if camera is switched on to fully automatic program mode.

The display appears as follows:

and this is what it means:

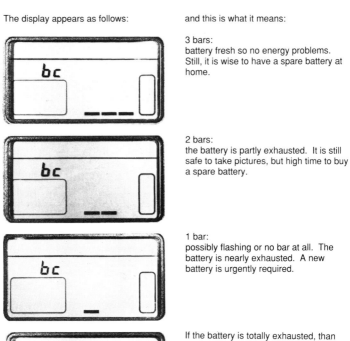

3 bars:
battery fresh so no energy problems. Still, it is wise to have a spare battery at home.

2 bars:
the battery is partly exhausted. It is still safe to take pictures, but high time to buy a spare battery.

1 bar:
possibly flashing or no bar at all. The battery is nearly exhausted. A new battery is urgently required.

If the battery is totally exhausted, than the panel stays blank.

The EOS takes any film – With or Without DX-Coding

Film Loading – Child's Play

To open the EOS, push the back cover latch down while pressing the back cover lock button. You can do this quite easily with just the index finger of your left hand. Naturally, you have to ensure that no partially-exposed film is in the camera but the LCD panel will keep your informed.

If you are not sure whether a film is loaded, check the film window at the rear on the left side. Most manufacturers provide film data in this position. Only if you are using a data back with your EOS 600 will this extra safety feature not be available.

- Insert the upper, flat end of the film cassette into the film chamber first. Pull the film leader across the shutter blinds until the end is aligned with the orange marker and at least one of the teeth of the sprocket wheel engages in the film perforations. Make sure that you do not touch the shutter blinds.
- Close back cover. If the camera is switched on the film will automatically be advanced to the first frame. In the LCD panel **1** will be displayed in the frame counter. If the camera is not switched on, simply turn the main switch in either direction from L and the rest will happen automatically. If the film is loaded properly and it is DX-coded, its speed will also be automatically read-in.

Now the camera is ready to take the first pictures. After each exposure the film is automatically wound to the next frame. After the 36th frame the film is automatically rewound into the cassette. The whole process is extremely fast and simple. One point to watch – the film leader must not get creased or badly bent, otherwise the film will not load properly.

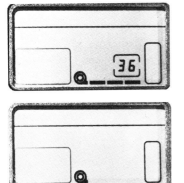

Film symbol with three bars: film is loaded in the camera – the back cover should not be opened.

Film symbol blinks: the film in the camera has been exposed and rewound. Open the back cover, remove the film and load a new one.

Total blank: careful this could mean –
1) camera switched off. No film loaded.
2) battery totally exhausted or no battery inserted (in this case the panel stays blank even if the camera is switched on) but a film could be loaded.

Types of Film for your EOS – with or without DX-coding

You can load any type of film into your EOS:
- The most economical buy (with certain reservations)
- The most commonly available brand names
- The make with the greatest variety of speeds and types
- The film with the largest number of exposures per roll

The nominal format of 35mm film is 24x36mm but the actual size of the frame is slightly smaller.

Different types of film		
Film	*Special types*	*Remarks*
Colour slide film	**daylight film** tungsten film infrared colour film instant film	usual type of film for use in artificial light only for experiments special type
Colour print film		
Black-and-white film	**usual types** litho film infrared film	reproduction experimental graphics
Black-and-white slide film		

Slide film is a reversal film that is processed and mounted in frames. Usually you send them off to a processing lab and they are returned framed and boxed. Photographic labs can also make colour prints from colour slides. However, the best results are achieved if you can do it yourself.

Black-and-white photography has its own particular charm, especially as the variety of b&w films has increased in recent years. Personally I am of the opinion, however, that it makes sense only to use b&w print film if you intend to process and print the pictures yourself. Printing of b&w negatives is very simple these days and it is also quite quick.

All films have another, very important property: speed.

- Films with slow speed require a lot of light, are very finely-grained and bear a small number to identify their low speed rating, e.g. ISO 25/15°.
- Films of high speed require less light, possess larger grain and therefore the pictures appear not so sharp, and are identified by a large number, e.g. ISO 400/27°.

ISO Film Speeds			
slow	*average*	*fast*	*very fast*
6/9°	**80**/20°	**250**/25°	**1250**/32°
8/10°	**100**/21°	**320**/26°	**1600**/33°
10/11°	**125**/22°	**400**/27°	**2000**/34°
12/12°	**160**/23°	**500**/28°	**2500**/35°
16/13°	**200**/24°	**640**/29°	**3200**/36°
20/14°		**800**/30°	**4000**/37°
*****25**/15°		**1000**/31°	**5000**/38°
32/16°			*6400/39°*
40/17°			
50/18°			
64/19°			

*The listed speeds are those that can be programmed into the EOS 600. The notations printed in italics can only be programmed by hand, the other speeds are read-in automatically or can be entered by hand. For reasons of space, the LCD panel always shows only the first part of the notation. This is printed in bold in the table.

These notations are the ISO values (International Standard Organisation) which is made up of two parts. The first part is the former ASA (American Standard), a doubling in the number means a doubling of the film speed. The second part corresponds to the old German DIN values (Deutsche Industrie Norm). In the DIN notation an increase of 3 units corresponds to a doubling of the film speed. Whenever space demands, manufacturers leave off the oblique stroke and the second part of the notation, using the former ASA value only. This is quite sufficient and satisfactory for our purposes.

The film speed range that can be programmed in the EOS is in fact larger than the actual speeds generally offered. The slowest films that are used these days are ISO 25/15° slide film (Kodachrome 25) and colour print film (Ektar 25). Both of these films are very fine grained and slower films are not available. The fastest film available is the black-and-white print film Kodak T-Max 3200. Generally you get better results if you overexpose this film slightly, 1600/33° should produce good results. There are also some colour films available with a speed of ISO 1600, which can be used in very poor lighting conditions. Compared with the slowest film rating of ISO 25, the ISO 1600 film is 64-times as fast! Naturally, the resolution of such a fast film will suffer! On the other hand, you can take snapshots in situations where otherwise you would have to keep your camera stowed away in your bag.

DX-coding is provided as a matter of course for most standard film types. This is the chess-board pattern on the film cassette, which carries the film speed information that is automatically read-in to the exposure control.

Automatic Programming of Film Speed

Generally you don't need to enter the film speed into your EOS 600. In case of doubt, check the film cassette. If you can see a bar code behind the slit where the film leader protrudes, and behind that the above mentioned chess-board pattern, than the film is encoded. Should an uncoded film be loaded into the EOS, a warning will flash in the LCD panel.

You load the film into the EOS in the usual way, taking care not to touch the shutter blinds, ensuring that the film lies completely flat with the perforations engaged in the teeth of the toothed wheels and the film leader touching the orange marker on the right side. Close the camera back and switch the camera on. The film will be wound automatically to the first frame. During the process the automatically read-in film speed appears in the LCD panel. This disappears as soon as the film has been moved to the firstf frame. If, on the other hand, the film speed cannot be read into the exposure system, perhaps because there is no DX-code, then the legend ISO will continue to flash in the panel to remind you to enter the value manually. The EOS is programmed to read-in automatically speeds of between 25/15° ISO and 5000/38°.

Film Speed Check – Film Speed Correction

To set the film speed we need to open the small cover at the rear of the functions which are not used very often. In order that the film speed cannot be changed inadvertently, an additional safety measure is provided; you have to press simultaneously two buttons – the yellow and the blue, making sure the main switch is turned to **((.))** or to **A**.

Film Speed Setting and Film Speed Control in the LCD Panel

- *Main switch to **((.))** or to **A**.*
- *Open cover at rear of camera*
- *Simultaneously press yellow and blue buttons.*

*The programmed ISO value (e.g. **ISO 100**) appears for about 8 sec. in the panel.*

Manual Override of Film Speed

With the ISO value displayed in the panel, turn the input dial to change the film speed to the required value.

*The entry of film speed is the only value that can be entered for both main switch positions **((.))** and **A**, and which is not cancelled or changed when the main switch is set to the green rectangle for automatic shooting.*

When is it necessary to use the manual override for film speed – i.e., when do we use film speed correction?

- If the film does not bear a speed code.
- If the film is to be processed differently from that required for the nominal film speed (pushed processing of colour slides or black-and-white film).
- If you prefer to use the automatic program mode for most situations (main switch to green rectangle) and exposure compensation is necessary for a sequence of shots.
- If you wish to make exposure compensations at 1/3-stop intervals. The film speed setting is in 1/3-stop intervals but the exposure compensation override is only possible in 1/2-stop steps.
- If the whole film is supposed to be over- or underexposed by a certain amount.

The last-mentioned case is the most important one. However, I would recommend that you make an exposure test with the film you are going to use before effecting any general exposure compensations.

The Greek singer Glykeria in concert. The film ISO 3200 exposed at ISO 800 for better resolution. The automatically-programmed film speed had to be manually reset.

Rewinding Partially-Exposed Film – Reloading Partially-Used Film

Occasionally it is necessary to remove a partially-exposed film from the camera and to change it for another, perhaps also partially exposed, film. It may be necessary to change the film for a faster one or a colour film for a black-and-white film. The EOS 600 is particularly suited for this as it is possible to change a film without losing a single frame.

However, first it is necessary to perform a certain adjustment to the basic programming of the EOS 600, which, once done, will remain effective. In the standard program the EOS 600 will rewind the film completely into the cassette. To re-use a partially-exposed film, the film leader must not be completely retracted into the cassette. To reprogram the camera you have to:

- Set main switch to one of the "on" positions.
- Lift the cover at the rear of the camera and simultaneously press the blue and black buttons. In the bracketed box of the LCD panel the number **1** will be displayed for 8 seconds.
- Keeping the buttons pressed, turn the input dial to display the number **2**.
- Press the partial metering button for a black bar to appear in front of the number **2**.

The display confirms that the EOS 600 is programmed to leave the film leader protruding from the cassette after rewinding.

Removing Partially-Exposed Film (from a reprogrammed EOS 600)

- *Read frame number off LCD panel*
- *Note frame number on film cassette or box*
- *Lift cover at rear of camera and press the black button – the film will be automatically rewound.*
- *Put film into box making sure that the leader is not kinked.*

Loading Partially Used Film

- *Read frame number off film cassette or box.*
- *Load film as usual, allowing automatic film transport to advance film to frame No. 1.*
- *Set EOS 600 to manual operation.*
- *Keep light from front of lens with cap and release shutter repeatedly until the required frame number is displayed in the LCD panel.*

Handling Lenses

Removing a Lens from the Camera Body

The lens release button is situated on the left next to the lens bayonet. This is a large, easily-accessible button which has to be pressed and then the lens can be turned anti-clockwise and removed. Note: never stand the lens bayonet-side down, this could damage the electrical contacts. Always attach both the rear and the front lens caps when the lens is not in use.

Attaching a Lens

Align the red dot on the camera with the red dot on the lens. Then gently push it in and turn clockwise until it clicks into place.

Manual and Automatic Focusing (AF)

The autofocus mode functions quickly and precisely with EOS cameras because each lens is equipped with its own AF motor. The focus mode switch on the lens allows you to select either autofocus or manual focus.

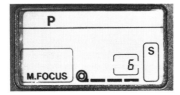

LCD panel showing manual focus

Zoom lenses with long focal lengths and macro facilities have a range limiter which divides the focusing range between AF macro to infinity and AF 2m to infinity.

When shooting distant subjects with focusing distances of 2m and further, it prevents the focusing mechanism having to traverse the entire focusing range from close-up to infinity, which is time and energy consuming.

Change-over to manual focusing is advisable if:

• The lens is supposed to be focused on infinity;
• A large focusing range between macro and infinity has to be bridged;
• If subject contrast and structure make it difficult for the AF mechanism to find the correct focus

EF 35-105mm, f3.5-4.5 zoom set to AF mode. If the focusing mode is changed to **M**, the lens has to be focused manually.

Fast Shutter Speeds and a Securely Supported Camera ensure Sharp Pictures

The faster the shutter speed, the sharper the pictures taken with a hand-held camera

The proportion of sharp pictures has increased in recent years. This may be partly due to autofocus cameras, but I think the availability of program modes in modern cameras is the real reason. Most people who photograph mainly with program mode are not even aware what shutter speeds they are using. Before the advent of program modes it used to be the fashion to use relatively slow shutter speeds; 1/60th or 1/30th sec for hand-held photography. The idea was to be able to stop down as much as possible to obtain as large a depth of field as the situation would allow. But even the greatest depth of field is no good if the picture is unsharp because of camera shake!

Some people maintain that they have a really steady hand and can use shutter speeds of 1/60th or even 1/15th sec in hand-held shooting. However, if you heed my advice and use, if at all possible, shutter speeds of 1/250th sec and faster, but in any case never slower than 1/125th sec, then you should always have sharp pictures. If you don't believe me,

When the camera is hand-held, as far as possible never give an exposure longer than 1/125th sec. When it is necessary to do so, find a support for your arms, such as the railings of the bridge in the foreground.

take a series of shots at different shutter speeds and compare the results.

If the lighting conditions are good, the EOS program mode will generally select shutter speeds of between 1/500th and 1/250th sec. In this case your pictures will definitely be sharp If you want to make sure that the program mode has sufficient scope to select fast enough shutter speeds, use a slightly faster film.

As soon as the program mode is forced to select slower shutter speeds than are reasonably safe for hand-held shooting, the camera will warn you by an audible alarm. The exposure control is programmed according to the well-tried rule that shutter speeds should not exceed the reciprocal of the focal length of the lens in mm, namely:

1/30th sec for a 24mm lens,
1/60th sec for a 50mm lens, and
1/125th sec for a 105mm lens.

Use of a Tripod

The use of tripods seems to be in fashion again. I often observe people arranging a tripod in front of an interesting building or some other feature, carefully setting up a shot with the self-timer so that they can include themselves in the picture.

Generally speaking you should always use a tripod for shutter speeds of 1/60th sec and slower. For a shutter speed of 1/8th sec the use of a tripod is an absolute must. If you buy a tripod, it has to be of good, rigid construction. Sometimes it is better to rely on a sturdy table-top or clamp-on tripod rather than a rickety full-size one. Extendable tripods have to be rather heavy; lighter models tend to vibrate and shake easily and there is no point in using them.

If you support your EOS 600 on a sturdy tripod, you can risk releasing by the shutter release button, even if you select a long exposure. If you fear that the pressure on the release button could upset both the camera and the tripod, then it is better to release by self-timer. It is not possible to attach a cable release to the EOS 600 but remote release 60T3 can be used. However, to attach this remote release you also need the additional handgrip GR 20. Handgrip GR 20 is different from the standard handgrip GR 30 in so far as it has a socket for the remote release. I would much prefer it if the EOS 600 were equipped with both handgrip GR 20 and remote release as standard. The "60" in the 60T3 indicates that the cable of the remote release is 60cm long. Canon offer extension cables up to 10m. The release on the hand unit is a two-stage switch, similar to the one on the camera itself; first pressure point for metering/focusing, and limit stop for shutter release. If you use the long exposure setting (bulb), you can lock the shutter in the open position by sliding the release sideways in the pressed-in position. The shutter can be closed only if the release button is moved back.

A Reasonable Compromise: Substitute Support Aids

Not so long ago I carried a rather heavy tripod for a 150km trip through the Greek mountains. This is not always possible and certainly not very often convenient. If the light is poor and even a fast film is insufficient, and a flash unsuitable or not powerful enough, then you may be forced to use shutter speeds between 1/60th and 1/8th sec without a tripod. In this case you will have to look for some other form of support – the back of a chair, a balustrade, a wall, a fence or the shoulder of a friendly passer-by. If no rigid surface can be found, it helps to lean, with legs firmly planted on the ground, against a wall, a tree, or a lamp-post. What is important is to support your hands because they hold the camera. Sometimes I crouch down and support my hands on my knees, or kneel down on one leg with the other bent as this presents a very steady support for arms and camera.

The EOS is firmly supported against a wall, the release effected by remote release. With luck you may get sharp pictures with shutter speeds as slow as 1/2 or even 1 second. Don't forget to put the cover over the eyepiece.

If the Audible Warning of the EOS is too noisy

Early one morning I found myself on the Pilion, a heavily wooded peninsula on the Eastern Greek coastline. In the East the sun rose above the Aegean Sea. I found a subject that looked promising. However, the light was still insufficient even for the fast film that I was using and the EOS 600 indicated a rather slow shutter speed by its sequence of bleep tones, which was the signal to start the whole dawn chorus! However, if I had tried to take some pictures in a festive concert hall, I doubt whether the serious listeners of some classical masterpiece would have appreciated it so much. In this case it is better to silence the EOS.

• Either turn the main switch to position **A**. The EOS is switched on and all additional program variations are activated, but both the camera-shake warning and confirmation that AF mode has been set are de-activated. If you change over to **((.))** or the green rectangle, then the audible signals will again be activated.

- Or turn the main switch to any one of the three "on"positions. Then open the switch cover at the rear of the camera and simultaneously press the black and blue buttons. In the LCD panel the number **1** is displayed in the frame. Keep the two buttons pressed and turn the input dial until the number **6** is shown. Now press the partial metering button on the right of the viewfinder and a bar symbol will appear in front of the number **6**. To cancel the function the partial metering button has to be pressed again.

This procedure cancels the audible camera-shake warning both in the **((.))** and the green rectangle positions. The single bleep tone for AF confirmation is still activated. If you choose this option you have to be careful as you will not be warned of possible camera-shake. The constant bleeping may be quite unnerving, particularly if you are shooting from a tripod, but it performs a useful function in many situations.

Summary of the 7 Custom Function Controls that can be programmed into the EOS 600

These are the options:

There are 7 custom function controls that are possible with the EOS 600 which are not available on the earlier models: 650, 620, 750 and 850.

Input	*Result*
1	*automatic film rewinding de-activated*
2	*film leader is not retracted into cassette when film is rewound*
3	*automatic reading-in of films cancelled*
4	*autofocus function is started only if partial metering button is pressed*
5	*in **M** (manual operation) the functions of the input dial and the **M** button are interchanged*
6	*audible warning for danger of camera-shake is de-activated*
7	*subsequent manual correction of autofocus setting for certain lenses*

All functions (with the exception of Nos. 4, 5 and 7) are operative in the three "on" positions.

All functions can be activated in the following way:
- Switch the EOS 600 on – to green rectangle, **((.))**, or **A**.
- Open the switch cover at the rear of the camera and simultaneously press the black and blue buttons. The number **1** is displayed for about 8 seconds in the LCD panel.
- Turn the input dial clockwise until the required number is displayed.
- Activate the required function with the appropriate number by pressing the partial metering button. A bar appears in front of the box to show that this function is activated.

To cancel a programmed function, the appropriate number has to be displayed, as previously, in the LCD panel and the partial metering button pressed again. The bar will disappear to indicate that the function is cancelled.

This is the display panel after the black and the blue buttons under the cover at the rear of the camera are pressed. Program functions 2 to 7 are recalled by turning the input dial.

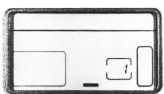

The display for custom function 1. The bar in front of the number shows that the function is activiated.

Custom Function 1 – de-activating automatic film rewinding

After the 36th frame, film transport stops. With this function activated the film is not automatically rewound.

Custom Function 2 – the film leader is left to protrude from the cassette

This function leaves the film leader protruding from the cassette when the film has been rewound. This is a very useful function. The protruding film leader helps to prevent stray light entering the film cassette, moreover, it allows a partially-exposed film to be rewound and reloaded into the camera. Naturally, you will have to identify a partially-exposed film by noting down the frame number. A completely exposed film should also be identified, maybe by kinking the film leader.

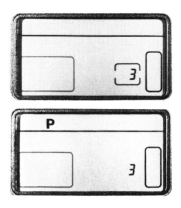

Please note: the top display shows that custom function 3 has been selected, the bottom display shows that the function has been activated.

Custom Function 3 – automatic film speed de-activated

The use of this function makes sense only if several films of the same speed are to be processed at ratings other than their nominal ISO speed.

Custom Function 4 – partial metering button activates AF mode

This de-activates the automatic focusing function when the shutter release button is lightly pressed but instead allows this function to work when the partial metering button is pressed. This is useful when working with partial metering as it avoids inadvertent triggering of the release, which does sometimes happen, when the only intention is to meter the subject. To use this control the main switch must be set to **((.))** or **A**. It will not work if the main switch is set to the green rectangle.

Custom Function 5 – shutter speed setting via input dial in manual mode only

In manual mode the shutter speed is selected by turning the input dial. The Manual Aperture Set button or the LCD panel illumination button is pressed and the input dial turned simultaneously to set the aperture, correct exposure being indicated by **oo** appearing in the LCD panel. With this alternative program the two operations are reversed – first the

Siesta time – with the day's work hanging out to dry. As the day is rather dark I used an exposure of –1/2 as this slight under exposure shows the colours to better effect.

aperture is preselected by the input dial, then the Manual Aperture Set button or the LCD panel illumination button is pressed while turning the input dial to select the appropriate shutter speed. This function is of interest particularly in situations where the combination of ambient lighting and flash illumination is the critical factor.

Custom Function 6 – audible camera-shake warning de-activated

I've already discussed when and how it might be important to silence the audible signal of the EOS 600, which warns you if the shutter speed is too slow for hand-held shooting. Don't forget, however, to cancel this alternative when silence is no longer needed otherwise there is no warning if the shutter speed falls below safe limits.

Custom Function 7 – Manual AF correction

This concerns only lenses with an ultrasonic motor. In the Canon range these are particularly fast lenses, i.e. lenses with large maximum apertures. When a subject is to be shown in sharp focus by reducing the depth of field to a very narrow region within the subject space, it can be useful to make minor manual corrections to the focus setting obtained by the AF mode. This function can be utilized only in main switch positions ((.)) and **A**.

1. Electronic input dial.
2. Shutter release.
3. Main switch.
4. Exposure correction.
5. Focus mode switch.
6. Back cover latch.
7. Bayonet release.
8. Depth-of-Field.
9. Manual aperture button.

A rooftop in Dinkelsbühl. The shiny roof tiles, wet from the rain, reflect the light sky like a mirror. A polarising filter reduces this effect and helps to restore the true colours of the roof. Below: the same subject without a filter.

Part III

Switch to green rectangle – fully automatic

Everything works automatically – super program mode

P means no-problem program

P is the abbreviation for program mode, which is your safeguard, rendering unintentional overexposure impossible, even in the presence of very bright highlights, and in unfavourable lighting conditions you will be warned of the danger of camera-shake.

The EOS 600 offers two versions of the P mode – one as a totally easy, totally automatic shooting mode (switch position green rectangle), and one with a variety of additional features (switch positions **((.))** and **A**).

Even the no-nonsense program mode of the EOS 600 (P mode) allows some program variations for the most important subject topics. These functions are very easy to control – i.e. it is impossible to do anything wrong.

Importance of the Main Switch Settings

Turning the main switch anti-clockwise; the green rectangle points upwards and the EOS 600 is set to fully automatic program mode. There is no need to take any notice of the displays because it is impossible to do anything wrong. In case the light is insufficient, the camera will warn you by a audible signal.

Turning the main switch clockwise; now the displays in the viewfinder have to be checked. Additional functions, such as exposure compensation or multiple exposures can be activated.

Only two things need to be considered when you are in fully automatic program mode:

• Check that the focus mode slide switch on the lens is set to AF.

Turn the main switch anti-clockwise to display the green rectangle on top. The EOS 600 is now set to fully automatic program mode.

- If the **P** in the LCD panel flashes, simultaneously press the mode button and turn the input dial two notches anti-clockwise. Repeat this until the **P** stops flashing.

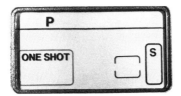

LCD panel for program mode. This display is shown for fully automatic program mode and also when all special functions are activated.

Data To Keep You Informed – Audible and Visual

Audible warning signal – danger of camera-shake

The EOS emits a bleeping signal to warn that the light is insufficient, despite fully open aperture, for the exposure control to set a sufficiently fast shutter speed. Therefore you have to:
- Use a tripod
- Support your arm/camera in some way
- Use flash
- Switch on a powerful photographic light
- Use a faster lens
- Use a faster film

Under normal lighting conditions, outdoors in daylight, it is usually practicable and convenient to use a zoom lens, for example, the EF 35-70mm, $f3.5$-4.5 or the 35-105mm. If you want to take pictures indoors without using a tripod, then it would be better to use a faster, fixed focal length lens. If you have reached the limits for hand-held shooting with an $f3.5$ lens, you can still shoot away happily with the 50mm, $f1.0$.

As soon as a flash is attached, the warning signal will stop, at least as soon as the flash capacitor is charged up and ready to go and the camera computer takes note of the situation and sets a faster shutter speed.

Only One Bleep – Everything OK with Autofocus

When you press the release of the EOS 600 halfway, a clear, single audible tone indicates that the AF control managed to set the correct focus. Usually this is done very quickly in just a fraction of a second. If it takes a little longer then the lighting conditions are poor or insufficient, the AF metering field may not be pointed at a subject area with clear outlines, or the AF mode has to cover a large focusing range. Until the audible tone signals correct focus the AF mechanism is still trying to find it for the subject detail within the AF target field and the green dot in the viewfinder LCD panel flickers showing that the process has not been completed and the shutter cannot be released.

If the audible signal sounds then the focus has been set and remains set! This is important – the focus setting will be stored as long as the release is pressed halfway. Now you can:

1. Press the release completely to make the exposure. The detail at the centre of the viewfinder will be in sharp focus, as well as all the subject details that are contained within the depth of field.
2. Keep the release pressed halfway and swing the camera to either side. No audible signal so you release; the focus setting remains unchanged. The subject detail within the AF target field will still be shown in sharp focus but now it will no longer be at the centre of the frame. The centre could now be occupied by a blurred section of background.
3. Take your finger off the release. The focus setting is cancelled. As soon as the release is pressed halfway down again, the AF mechanism will restart the focusing sequence, confirming correct focusing with an audible signal.

The Most Important Information is Displayed in the Viewfinder

I find it very convenient that all the relevant information lights up below the viewfinder screen after the shutter release is pressed halfway, and stays illuminated for 6 seconds.

Above: spontaneous snapshot with the EOS 600 set to fully automatic **P** mode.
Left: viewfinder LCD panel showing shutter speed of 1/125th, aperture of ƒ2.8 and in-focus indicator

In the fully-automatic program mode with the main switch at the green rectangle position the display shows, from left to right, the shutter speed, aperture setting, flash symbol –which only appears if a system flash is attached and is fully charged – and the AF indicator. This green dot flickers while the AF system tries to find correct focus; it stays illuminated if correct focus is set and stored.

Four further displays are available in switch positions **((.))** and **A**.

It is possible to restrict information to essentials because it can be complemented by audible signals and all other information can be read off the main LCD panel.

LCD Panel: three types of information

The information in this panel is supplied in three different ways:
I.   display of activated functions/information
II. permanent information
III. special programming aids

I. Displays activated by pressing the release:
These are the same displays that are also visible in the viewfinder – namely shutter speed and aperture value. The panel has no in-focus indicator (this function is indicated by the audible signal instead). Flash-ready is also not indicated, as this can be read off the flashgun. However, any changes in aperture and shutter speed settings when a readily charged system flashgun is attached are displayed when the release is pressed. The displays are not really needed in fully automatic program mode, only perhaps if you are using the long exposure sequence and a tripod.

LCD panel when release is pressed half-way; shutter speed and aperture appear.

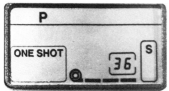

LCD panel when main switch is set at the green rectangle but the release not pressed.

II. Permanent displays:

P stands for program mode. No changes can be effected.

ONE SHOT means focusing with focus lock. If the focus mode selector on the lens is set to manual, M.FOCUS is displayed.

Nos. 1 – 36 in the box indicate the frame of the film that is going to be exposed.

S means that film advance is set to single exposure; i.e. for each exposure the release has to be pressed. This setting is also retained in program mode.

Film symbol with 3 bars means that a film is loaded. This symbol flickers during transport/rewinding. If a rewound film is in the camera, then the symbol only flashes. If the film is not loaded properly, then the three bars flash.

III. Special Programming/Auxiliary Displays:

• Battery check display appears when the black button, behind the switch cover at the rear of the camera, is pressed.

• Input of a Custom Function Control. When the blue button as well as the black button is pressed the number **1** appears in the frame counter of the LCD panel. Turn the input dial to select the required number, from 1 to 7, and set it by pressing the partial metering button.

When a Custom Function Control is selected, a number is displayed in the box, bottom right, otherwise the LCD panel is blank.

• Input of Program Image Control. By pressing the MODE button, on the left shoulder of the camera, the number **1** is displayed in the frame counter of the LCD panel. It is now possible to select a program variation between 1 and 7 by turning the input dial. The **P** flashes continuously as a reminder that the standard mode is not in use.

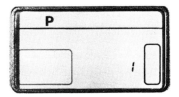

When a Programmed Image Control option is selected, a number without a box is displayed.

Focusing – AF (autofocus) or M (manual)

Manual Focusing

Some people claim to have problems with automatic focusing. I have had the chance to use several autofocus cameras and despite my initial scepticism and, I must confess, a certain resistance, I have had no difficulty in adjusting to this new facility. On the contrary, I am beginning to find the AF facility an almost essential feature. However, I can imagine that some of you feel entirely different about this. I blame advertising for asserting that autofocus is an entirely unsupervised function and the photographer does not have to do anything. This is nonsense of course. Proper use of the autofocus facility is just as skilful as manual focusing. If, initially, you have problems with the autofocus, switch it off. After all, this is why the slide switch on the lens has been provided. With the focus mode switch set to **M**, use the knurled ring on the front of the lens to focus manually. You will soon realize that focusing manually with an AF camera is not much different from using a conventional camera without autofocus facility.

On the other hand, there is one advantage over conventional cameras – the green in-focus indicator in the viewfinder and the audible signal.

Focusing manually or by AF function – that is the question – or no question at all! In fact, this picture was by AF function. The head of the bird was at the centre of the frame and the AF mechanism caught it clearly and precisely.

A very convenient subject. Focusing can be done from the centre of the area as the whole subject is situated in this focusing plane. Presented with a subject like this you can push the release button fully, the shutter will release as soon as the AF mechanism has indicated correct focus. Should you wish, you could always re-align the camera for better framing.

You focus the lens as usual, press the release halfway to take the exposure reading and, if correct focus has been achieved, the green in-focus indicator lights up and the audible tone gives a short signal. This is a useful and additional check to the bright image on the focusing screen. If you are wearing glasses then I would recommend you to fit an eyesight correction lens on the eyepiece.

As soon as you move the camera and the subject detail at the centre of the frame is no longer in sharp focus, the green in-focus indicator will disappear. If you adjust the focus to the changed situation, the green in-focus indicator will appear again plus the confirmative bleep.

Please note: in M.FOCUS mode the exposure mode adjusts continually to the changing lighting conditions outlined by the particular frame, i.e. the exposure settings are not stored.

Fully Automatic Focusing

Not a single picture of the first three rolls of film I took with the EOS 600 was unsharp. This came as no great surprise to me, after all, I had some experience with autofocus as I used the EOS 620 before the EOS 600.

To start with you would be well advised to practise with stationary subjects that possess a reasonably well-defined light-dark structure, perhaps a fence, a tiled roof, brickwork, the branches or foliage of a tree. The majority of everyday subjects are quite suitable for AF focusing. Place the important subject detail within the AF target field of the focusing screen and press the release halfway down. With a soft sound the lens will adjust its focusing setting and the green in-focus indicator below the focusing screen flickers. If the subject detail is not very bright or possesses poorly-defined features, then the autofocus may have to search for the correct focus and the lens tube will be moving to and fro, traversing the focusing range. The whole process generally takes no longer than 1/50th to at most 1/2 second. Correct focus setting will then be confirmed by a short bleep and the continuously-lit green in-focus indicator.

Now you have two choices:

- Either you press the release halfway down, then push it all the way down to take the picture;
- Or your finger has already descended heavily and the shutter is automatically released, as soon as the electronics issue the all-clear.

Now let's deal with subjects that need a little more thought in the focusing and framing. Let's assume you are interested in a shrub with a brick wall a few metres behind it. If the AF target field covers a branch of the shrub and also the outlines of some bricks in the background, the AF mechanism will move between the subject planes, from the twig to the brick and back again, not knowing which focusing plane to choose. The first time this happened to me I did not quite know how to deal with it and turned the lens to manual focusing. Now I know better. The AF mechanism works perfectly even in situations like this as long as the AF target field is occupied by a large proportion of the important subject detail. Describing the process is more complicated than actually doing it, all it takes is a little practice. Practice is important at the beginning – after all, I did warn you that your first two lithium batteries would not last very long!

I hope you noticed that I did not say the subject detail has to completely cover the AF target field. This is not necessary and not always a very good idea. If the subject has good contrasts and well-defined lines then it works well; on the other hand, if it is poorly defined the AF mechanism will not be able to find a suitable point to base its measurements on. In this case it is a good idea to include an edge – with the necessity of including a little background – and as long as the relative proportion of background is small this method will work perfectly.

I am sure that I am not going to surprise you when I say to focus on moving objects is a lot more difficult; this applies both to manual focusing and to autofocus.

It happens quite often in close-ups that foreground and background both try to be in sharp focus. You have to make sure that the focusing plane is situated within the desired subject detail.

However, if you put the camera to your eye because you noticed an interesting scene in a market square, you will have a better chance of getting a sharp picture with autofocus than with manual focusing. Moreover, you can improve your chances considerably by prefocusing the lens to the approximate distance. For example, if I hope to catch a gesticulating trader at his market stall, about 6m from my camera, then the lens has to bridge a considerable focusing path if it happens to be focused at 50cm; this could take as long as 1/2 or even one full second. In such situations I prefocus the lens manually to the approximate distance and let the autofocus adjust the exact focus by bringing my subject into the AF target field. Now the focusing process takes just a fraction of a second.

Prefocusing is a good method for objects moving at a moderate speed (animals, athletes). If you are trying to catch a jogger but have the feeling that his effort-strained face may have already left the focusing plane after you received the confirmative bleep, then you will have to quickly let go of the release button and press it halfway down again to allow the AF mode to refocus. This action is necessary in such cases because the focus setting is stored as long as the release is kept pressed halfway down.

For fast moving subject you have the choice of using either manual focusing or changing over to SERVO.

What is important though, is to be able to use either mode, as both will produce perfect results provided you use them properly. The EOS 600 offers both facilities and this is only right as there is every justification for both.

The Elusiveness of Sharpness

It is not always correct to place the focusing plane in the foreground. Sometimes it is more effective to place the focusing plane in the middle distance or even background. A landscape may gain a particular atmosphere if it is framed by unsharply-defined branches in the foreground. To focus correctly in this case you point the camera at a piece of landscape in the background; this works very well and details around the edge of the frame will not interfere with the AF mechanism as long as you can point the camera so that more than half the AF target field covers background details.

ONE SHOT Focusing means Focus Lock

Somebody I know asserted that it was not possible to produce unsharp pictures with the AF facility activated if the photographer did not manage to adjust for the correct focusing plane. I absolutely disagree with this assertion. It is just as easy to produce unsharp pictures with

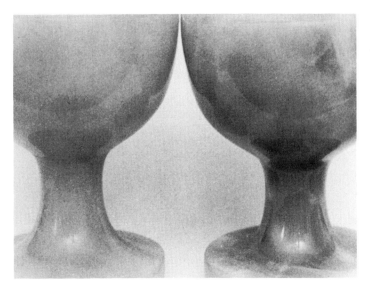

The subject itself lacks any clear detail. Even if the AF target field were located precisely on the subject the AF mechanism would be unable to focus on it. In this case it is better to choose the outlines of the goblets but to make sure that more than half the subject lies within the target fields.

autofocus as with manual focusing. Simply focus on a subject in the close range, keep the release pressed half-way, swing the camera round, point it at a further subject and release. As the focus setting was stored for the close subject, the picture will be unsharp. If, however, you released the button and again pressed it half-way down, then the AF mechanism would have taken a new reading and confirmed this by the audible signal.

I have cited the above example to explain what happens when we talk of focus lock – if we keep the release pressed halfway down, the focus setting is stored.

- Focus lock is provided to retain the focus setting for subjects that do not lie at the centre of the frame.
- To reposition a sharply-focused detail from the centre of the frame towards the edge of the picture means moving the camera round after focusing – to the right or left, depending on how the image needs to be composed, or even up or down.

What would happen if the AF mechanism did not store the focus setting and if it always automatically readjusted it for the detail at the centre of the frame?

How different the impressions from these two pictures. The only difference between them is that the focusing plane has been shifted from the foreground to the background.

- In this case the focus setting would always be adjusted every time the camera is moved.
- The focusing plane would always adjust for a moving subject.
- Only subjects at the centre of a frame could be shown in sharp focus.

You will pleased to hear that the EOS 600 can be changed over to focus continuously – the AI SERVO setting. However, this facility is not available in standard program mode.

The AF mode Baffled – What Now?

There are four types of subjects that the AF facility cannot cope with. The AF motor will push the lens mechanism through the entire focusing range, from close-up to infinity, and back again. Then it will give up and stop.

Case 1:
The metered surface is quite light, without or with very little structure. This type of subject is the most common one that presents problems. Amongst these are long distance shots, landscapes in the fog, plain featureless surfaces and similar objects.
Remedy. Set the focus to infinity. In most cases this is correct as it is usually a subject situated some distance away.

Case 1: A low contrast landscape; change to manual focusing and set lens to infinity.

Case 2:

EOS in the normal, horizontal format position. The AF target field is confronted with horizontal lines only. The AF mechanism is unable to cope with subjects of this kind as it can only focus on vertical and contrasty lines.

Remedy: Turn the camera to upright format and take the picture this way, or at least take the measurement in upright format, keeping the release pressed halfway; now the EOS 600 can be returned to the horizontal format position and the exposure made.

Case 2: horizontal parallel structures at the centre of the frame; the AF mechanism can only focus on vertical lines. Turn the camera to upright format to focus.

Case 3:

EOS in upright format and the AF mechanism is confused by vertical lines in the AF target field.

Remedy: Turn the camera to horizontal format and take the picture this way, or allow the AF mode to set the focus and re-align to upright format.

Case 4:

Subjects are staggered towards the background. Foreground and background vie with each other for which should be the one that the camera focuses on.

Remedy:Point camera so that a large enough proportion of the subject detail that you are interested in is brought into the AF target field. You may have to change to manual focusing.

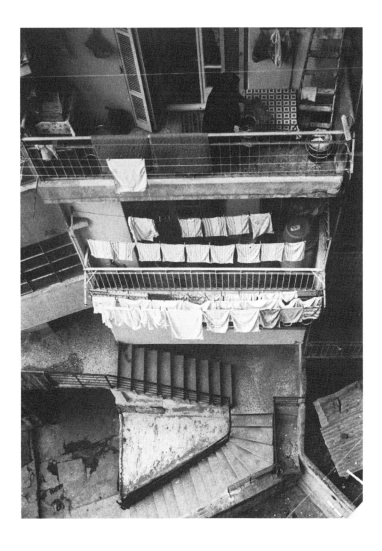

Case 3: in the upright format the AF target field covers a lot of horizontal lines; turn the camera to horizontal format position, move it slightly to avoid too much railing, allow the AF function to set the focus, change the camera back to upright format and take the shot.

Case 4: critically frames subject. A cypress tree in the background was used to allow the AF mechanism to set the focus.

Case 5:

Two ill-defined focusing planes vie with each other for attention e.g. a dirty reflecting surface and a reflected image, a lake with a reflection, etc. **Remedy**: Set the focus manually.

Case 6:

A scene in the dusk/dawn or in the dark. There is insufficient light for the AF mode to function.

Remedy: Change to manual focus or, better still, attach a system flashgun. The infrared metering beam of the flashgun will project a striped pattern onto the subject surface which the AF mechanism uses to take a reading. The actual picture need not be taken with the flash.

Case 5: this type of subject is too confusing for any automatic focusing system. In this case it is better to change to manual focusing.

Case 6: if it is too dark then the infrared metering flash of the flash can help with focusing, whether or not the final picture is to be taken with flash.

Exposure by Program Mode

Program Mode Excludes the Possibility of Over-Exposure

Program mode, just like the other automatic shooting modes of the EOS 600, is capable of preventing the likelihood of overexposure because it is programmed to increase the shutter speed, to 1/2000th sec, and stop down the aperture corresponding to any increase of illumination intensity. Overexposure is therefore only possible if one is using a very fast film in the brightest daylight.

The determining factor for the function is the focal length of the lens. Let's assume we are dealing with a poorly-lit subject that gradually becomes brighter. The standard program mode will ensure that the aperture stays fully open and only the shutter speed will be gradually increased. This continues with increasing brightness until the shutter speed is equal to the reciprocal value of the focal length of the attached lens in mm; therefore if a 30mm lens is used it is 1/30th sec; or a 50mm lens, 1/60th sec; or a 100mm lens, 1/125th sec, etc.

These are the shutter speeds that represent the safe limit for hand-held photography, up to which camera-shake warnings will be sounded. If the subject brightness continues to increase, then the program will alternately increase the shutter speed and stop down the aperture.

Details of heavily used and corroded objects – an agricultural machine with the façade of a house in Schleswig Holstein in the background. (Pages 87 and 88). A drum of diesel fuel (page 89, top) and a digger (page 89, bottom and page 90).

The choice of framing, the determination of the depth of field, the carefully selected focusing plane stored by AF focus lock, produce interesting compositions in shape and colour. The pictures on pages 87, 88, and 89 (top) were taken on Kodachrome 64 film, the pictures on page 89 (bottom) and page 90 were on Agfachrome CR100 film.

Program mode aperture/shutter speed combinations with increasing subject brightness

Focal length 30mm, maximum aperture f4

aperture	4	4	4	4	4.5	4.5	5.6	5.6
speed	1/10	1/15	1/20	1/30	1/30	1/45	1/45	1/60

aperture	6.7	6.7	8	8	13	13	16	16
speed	1/60	1/90	1/90	1/125	1/125	1/180	1/180	1/250

aperture	19	19	22	22	22	22	22	22
speed	1/250	1/350	1/350	1/500	1/750	1/1000	1/1500	1/2000

Focal length 100mm, maximum aperture f5.6

aperture	5.6	5.6	5.6	5.6	5.6	6.7	6.7	8
speed	1/30	1/45	1/60	1/90	1/125	1/125	1/180	1/180

aperture	8	13	13	16	16	19	19	22
speed	1/250	1/250	1/350	1/350	1/500	1/500	1/750	1/750

aperture	22	22	22
speed	1/1000	1/1500	1/2000

Each subsequent exposure value corresponds to 50% more light.

For lenses with a longer focal length, the program mode chooses faster times and wider apertures. For shorter focal lengths preference is given to slower shutter speeds combined with smaller apertures.

Centre-weighted Metering Lock

In normal shooting mode the EOS 600 is set to integral metering. However, as it is assumed that for most subjects the most important details are placed at the centre of the frame, the metering results are centre-weighted, i.e. more emphasis is given to the lighting conditions at the centre and less towards the edge of the frame.

A slight pressure on the release button starts the metering process, the exposure control displays the calculated aperture and shutter speed in the viewfinder. This display stays lit for about 8 seconds after releasing the button, if the release is fully pressed home and the shot is taken, the display disappears immediately.

The exposure metering process continues to adjust its readings and as long as no correct focus is set the green in-focus indicator in the viewfinder flickers. You can check this by observing the aperture and shutter speed values in the display changing with the changing images captured within the frame. As soon as the bleep tone confirms correct focus and the in-focus indicator stays lit, the exposure setting is stored together with the focus setting. If the camera is now moved from side to side or up and down to change the framing and place the important subject detail off-centre, none of the stored settings will be changed as long as the release is held halfway down. We can make the exposure with the stored settings, or let go of the release to start another sequence.

Autofocus lock and exposure lock are interconnected. As long as the distance setting is stored, the exposure setting is stored as well. But as soon as the AF lock is released the exposure lock is also released.

Connecting the AF lock with the exposure lock is suitable for most photographic situations. However, there are times when this is not true. Let's take a situation where you try to capture a thunderstorm mood with dark clouds being driven by a high wind across the sky. The landscape seems to shake in the staccato of the changing light. In this case the exposure metering has to continually adjust until the moment when the shot is taken.

De-activate the AF facility by setting the slide switch on the lens to M and adjust the focus manually. In M.FOCUS mode the exposure lock is cancelled.

Creative Override Facilities in Exposure Metering

Small bright subjects in front of dark backgrounds present a problem

A large background with a relatively small, but very bright foreground confuses the exposure mode. The dark surfaces indicate that there is poor illumination and the exposure mode reacts to this by allowing a longer exposure which is too much for the bright foreground. The picture will be totally over-exposed. Print film may just about cope with this situation. With slide film the exposure has to be kept rather on the short side.

A brightly-lit area surrounded by dark shadows – this type of subject requires a considerable exposure compensation.

Small dark details in front of a bright background are just as awkward

A dark point in front of a light background is just as confusing for the exposure system. Now the tendency is to reduce the exposure. A black horse in a snow-covered field will definitely be very underexposed. In this case too, the photographer has to make compensations regardless of whether he uses slide or print film.

Solution: Partial Metering is the Key: Whenever the slide switch on the lens is set to AF the exposure is stored with the focus setting. In case our main subject occupies only a tiny fraction of the whole frame we could look for a substitute subject which we meter and focus on, keeping the release halfway pressed, then re-align the camera for the desired frame to take the picture. Example: a white church in dark woods, lit by a bright beam of sunlight at a far distance. The important subject is the church. To the left is a sunlit bank of clouds possessing the same brightness as the church. Solution: point camera at the clouds to take a meter reading! Keep release pressed and swing camera round to bring the church into the frame and release.

Solution: Exposure Lock independent of Focusing: Substitute metering means measuring another object in the same area as the subject you are interested in. In most cases it can be – and will be – desirable to memorize the focus setting as well. Now let's assume we want to take a rose, backlit, against a dark background with a macro lens. We could move close enough to the rose to take a reading for the exposure and move back again to get the desired framing. The stored exposure setting will be correct, only the focus will be completely out. What now? Well, we employ a little trick to outwit the EOS. Keeping the release pressed halfway, change the focus mode switch on the lens to M and correct the focus manually. The exposure setting will remain stored. I admit this sounds a little complicated but it is not so in practice. This method is not recommended in the camera manual but it is a perfectly legitimate method of outwitting the camera's pre-ordained functions.

Solution: Zoom Metering: With a zoom lens it is possible to adjust the exposure metering for a small subject area with activated AF function – provided, of course, you intend to take the picture at a longer focal length setting. Let's stay with the example of the rose against the dark background.
- Set lens to longest focal length setting
- Lightly press release, as soon as the bleep tone is sounded both exposure and focus settings are stored
- Keep release pressed halfway, adjust lens for the required focal length setting to show the rose against the dark background, and release!

Measuring the subject with extended zoom has the additional advantage that the focus setting is particularly precise.

Solution: Correction by Overriding Film Speed Setting: In principle we also have the possibility of overriding the film speed setting, by halving or doubling the film speed, for subjects where over- or underexposure is likely. But if you conclude that an exposure compensation for just one frame is a trifle too complicated with this method – set the main switch to **((.))** and use the exposure compensation facility.

It is different if you want to over- or underexpose the entire film. I tend to use a higher speed setting for slide films as a rule, i.e. instead of ISO 100, I use ISO 125. This makes my slides a shade darker, the colours a little more brilliant.

Apart from the above subjects, there are a whole range of flash subjects where some sort of exposure compensation is necessary.

Fully Automatic Flash - The Intelligent Automatic

Flash Exposure Metering – Through The Lens with System Flashguns

The special Canon EOS system flashguns are simply slid into the hot shoe of the EOS 600 and secured by the knurled knob. Flashguns made for the EOS system by other manufacturers have to be set to TTL (Through-The-Lens).

As an extra precaution – this is probably not necessary, but better safe than sorry – enter the film speed on the flashgun. The exposure and the distance setting are metered through the lens both in daylight conditions and in total darkness. This is surprisingly simple, with one provision however; in many situations an exposure compensation towards a slight underexposure is advisable. If a whole film is shot with flash it may be easier to override the film speed setting.

There is a type of flash illumination which is particularly uniform and subject-friendly, that is bounce flash. For this we turn the reflector of the flashgun at an angle, usually upwards towards the ceiling (this is not

Direct flash illumination:
the flash is mounted on top of the camera, and used as a direct frontal light.

The same subject, but this time with bounce flash. The reflector of the flashgun, again mounted on the hot shoe, was pointed towards the ceiling.

95

possible with all flashguns). The indirectly reflected light that bounces back from the ceiling provides a much softer, more even illumination, without the heavy shadows that characterize direct flash.

Infrared Distance Metering in Complete Darkness

There are many situations when a flash is required. The most obvious is when it is dark and it is difficult to see. In this case even the AF mechanism will be at a loss. For this reason EOS flashguns have a separate AF metering facility – the AF infrared metering flash. For flashguns of other manufacturers an AF metering flash unit may be purchased separately.

As soon as the flashgun is attached to your EOS 600, switched on and ready to shoot, the metering flash will automatically emit a striped pattern of infrared, if the metering sensor reports low level lighting conditions. This forms the basis for the AF metering and exposure control. The whole process is extremely fast – in the time it has taken you to read this paragraph you would have been able to take several pictures!

Beware the Night and Total Darkness: Exposure Compensation Necessary!

A large proportion of flash photographs – more than half, I would say – show a brightly-lit main subject in the foreground against a dark background. This happens for several reasons:

- The subject is placed against a dark background/landscape at night or in semi-darkness.
- The subject is placed in a room, relatively far away from the background. Due to the steep decline in light intensity with increasing distance, the background is left in the dark.
- The wall, curtain, or similar object behind the main subject is very dark.
- The subject is taken in daylight at close range and is heavily filled-in.

Perhaps you doubt what I say, but in all these situations the subject in the foreground would be overexposed. You may not always notice this, particularly if you are using black-and-white or colour print film. This type of film material accommodates a certain amount of overexposure and the results will still be quite acceptable. The situation is different with slide material when the overexposure is very obvious. The remedy is exposure compensation. If you are presented with one of the above situations, simply reprogram the film speed to twice the nominal value, e.g. ISO 200 instead of 100, or ISO 400 instead of 200.

Late Byzantine fresco in a church at Pilion, Greece. The church was locked and the windows boarded. I managed to take this picture, through a gap in the boards, with my EOS 600 and Speedlight 420EZ. I pointed it roughly at the picture and allowed the infra-red autofocus flash and automatic exposure to do the rest – not a bad result by any means.

Beware of Dark Subjects: Exposure Compensation!

I don't mean subjects in the dark, but darkly-coloured subjects – perhaps a black cat in the arms of a chimney sweep. Such black-on-black subjects confuse the exposure metering and it will allow too much exposure, thinking it a badly-lit normal subject. The picture will be overexposed, the colours will no longer be rich and dense, but greyish.

> *The majority of subjects that need flash need to be underexposed when slide film is used, sometimes by as much as a half to a whole f-stop.*

Important when the Light Fails: LCD Panel Illumination

If it is dark and you wish to refer to the LCD panel for some information, simply press the display panel illumination button on the top right of the camera back. This switches on a blue light for about 6 sec. To turn off within this time press the button again.

97

Programmed Image Control – Tailored For Each Subject

7 No-Risk, No-Problem, Preset Modes

The EOS 600 has a unique range of preset program modes. With the other EOS cameras the main switch had to be moved to the left to call up the special program functions. This meant a change over to a range of functions that offered special facilities but at the same time it necessitated vigilance by the photographer, as the special exposure programs could now allow incorrect exposure settings. It is possible to shoot without worry, and without even having to check the settings in the viewfinder, only as long as the main switch is turned to the green rectangle. The improvement offered by the EOS 600 is that the uncomplicated shooting in program mode is extended to suit particular subject groups, without the risk of doing anything wrong. Special functions, such as intentional over- or underexposure, multiple exposures or exposure bracketing are still not available in this mode. On the other hand, these special functions do not interfere in any way. Even if I choose the wrong program for a particular subject, say P4 Sports Program for a close-up of a flower, while it won't produce the world's greatest study of our indigenous flora, the result will at least be properly exposed and perfectly sharp.

P1 Standard Program Mode

Little more can be said about this program. This is the straight-forward mode for uncomplicated shooting. Which of the program variations is selected is visible in the LCD panel as long as the MODE button on the left camera shoulder is pressed.

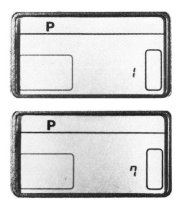

Basic setting for program variations

Program 7 – interior photography is selected. The display is visible only as long as the MODE button is kept pressed.

To select one of the possible settings, Programs 1 - 7, press the MODE button and simultaneously turn the input dial, which displays the numbers in turn in the bottom right-hand corner of the LCD panel. By selecting a number in the panel the appropriate program is activated. To cancel the selection, press the MODE button again and simultaneously turn the input dial to another number or to basic program (No. 1). As soon as the MODE button is released, the numbers disappear. If the **P** in the panel blinks, it indicates that one of the program variations between P2 and P7 is selected.

P2 Snapshot Program

The important thing with snapshots is that the AF function and exposure control adjust continuously for the changing conditions.

P2 control means the following:
- The focus setting continuously follows the subject (A1 SERVO), it even calculates – and this is a speciality introduced with the EOS 600 – the speed and direction of the subject and keeps on adjusting the focus setting right up to the time the shutter is released.
  No focus lock!
- The exposure program continuously adjusts for changing brightnesses almost instantaneously!
  No exposure lock!
- The usual shooting mode characteristics (the exposure curve for aperture/shutter speed is the same as for **P1**)
- By keeping the shutter release pressed, you can take a sequence of shots at a rate of up to 5 frames per second.

Please note: the important subject detail has to be at the centre of the frame as the focus setting adjusts for this area.

P3 Landscape Program

When taking landscapes a large depth of field is required, i.e. the aperture has to be stopped down as much as possible. This program is also suitable for town scenes and large interiors (camera on tripod).

P3 control means the following:
- AF mode with focus lock (as for P1)
- Exposure mode with exposure lock (coupled with AF lock), as for P1.
- Single frame shooting (as for P1)
- Exposure curve prefers smaller apertures, resulting in slower shutter speeds.

Choose Program Image Control 2 – always suitable for a quick snapshot.

Landscapes are always shown to advantage in Program Image Control 3.

For sport and play, choose Program Image Control 4.

P4 Sports Program

This special program for sports photography is similar to P2 – Snapshot Program. However, now the program allows for fast moving subjects; this program mode is also suitable for shooting animals in their natural habitat.

P4 control means the following:
• The new Focus Prediction continually tracks moving subjects (AI SERVO), it even calculates the speed and direction of them and keeps adjusting the focus setting.
  No focus lock!

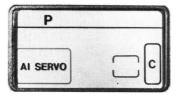

Display on the panel for program selection P4 (also P2). The **P** blinks.

• The exposure program continuously adjusts for changing brightnesses.
  No exposure lock!
• By keeping the shutter release pressed, you can take a sequence of shots at a rate of up to 5 frames per second.
• The exposure curve gives preference to fast shutter speeds resulting in wider apertures.

Please note: the important subject detail has to be at the centre of the frame – the focus setting adjusts for this subject area.

P5 Portrait Program

When taking portraits it is important to frame the subject to full advantage and to determine a narrow depth of field with precise focusing. At the same time it is important to be able to release quickly to capture a natural, unselfconscious expression.

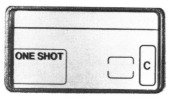

Display for P5 program selection

For portraits the EOS 600 provides Program Image Control 5.

P5 control means the following:
- AF control with focus lock.
- Exposure mode with exposure lock (coupled with AF lock).
- The exposure curve gives preference to fast shutter speeds resulting in wider aperture openings.
- By keeping the shutter release pressed, you can take a sequence of shots at a rate of up to 5 frames per second.

P6 Close-Up Program

For macro shots, perhaps a close-up of a flower, the most important subject detail which has to be correctly exposed usually lies at the centre of the frame. The close-up program takes this into account and disregards exposure readings from the edge of the frame.

P6 control means the following:
- AF control with focus lock.
- Automatic partial metering with exposure lock (coupled with AF lock)
- Single frame shooting (as for P1)
- Exposure curve favours smaller apertures, necessitating slower shutter speeds.

P7 Interiors Program

In interior photography we are usually faced with low-level lighting. The interior program considers this and selects suitable aperture/shutter speed combinations for shooting with or without a tripod or flash in interiors, outside at dusk and dawn and in poor lighting conditions generally.

P7 control means the following:
- AF control with focus lock.
- Exposure control with AF dependent exposure lock.
- Now the program curve follows similar characteristics as for Av mode, i.e. it selects a relatively large aperture and adjusts the shutter speed to suit the prevailing lighting conditions.
- Changing to flash: Shutter speeds are reduced (or, if long exposures would result in the absence of flash, the shutter speeds are increased). The aperture is stopped down as appropriate.
- Single frame shooting.

Flowers and similar close-ups are perfect with Program Image Control 6.

PART IV

The Ingenious Programs of the EOS 600

Main Switch Anti-Clockwise to ((.)) or A

Switch Position ((.))

Welcome to the circle of advanced EOS photographers!

You may be considered "advanced" once you have shot about a dozen films with the main switch set to the green rectangle. Although I can look back on a long career as a photographer, I too used only the program modes to start with and when taking snapshots I still prefer to choose the fully automatic setting. Meantime I have elected the **((.))** setting as my favourite one.

Main switch set to **((.))**. All functions are activated.

What now?

- All functions are fully activated.
- The input dial behind the release activates certain functions if one or two other buttons are pressed at the same time.
- So now we have to be careful not to turn the input dial inadvertently as something different will be activated in almost all the settings. Exactly what will happen has to be understood!
- The LCD panel keeps us informed of what has been selected. Now this information is really important and needs to be checked. In most cases it is not necessary to press the release to display the appropriate information.
- A few very important functions cause a visual warning to be displayed below the focusing screen when the release is pressed. For example, the ± symbol if an exposure compensation has been selected or a * if partial metering is chosen.
- All selections that were entered by pressing one or two buttons and simultaneously turning the input dial clockwise, can be cancelled by pressing the same button(s) again and turning the input dial anti-clockwise.

Retaining a special function:
*Switch camera off (main switch to position **L**). As soon as the camera is switched back to **((.))** or **A**, all previously-selected settings are activated again.*

Quick cancellation of all special functions:
*Turn main switch to green rectangle: All special functions are now cancelled even when the main switch is turned back to **((.))**. Exception: correction of automatically-read film speed, this is retained for the whole film.*

All special functions are retained when the EOS 600 is turned off – main switch to **L**. Main switch to green rectangle cancels all the settings.

In the **((.))** and the **A** shooting modes, the displays in the viewfinder and in the LCD panel have to be heeded. If a certain photographic situation is so fast moving that you are unable to consider properly all the settings and have no time to adjust anything, then it would be better to change over to the green rectangle!

Main Switch position A

The audible signal of the EOS 600 that confirms every successful focusing and warns every time the shutter speed seems too slow for hand-held shooting, is silenced in this setting. Otherwise there is no difference between this and the main switch setting **((.))**.

Main switch to **A**. All creative functions are activated except the audible warnings.

107

Occasionally there is a good reason for suppressing these audible warnings as I have explained already. However, I find that they are so valuable during shooting that I silence them only on the very rare occasions when this seems absolutely imperative.

Automatic Program Mode with Special Functions

This is the Way to Use It

If I switch on the EOS 600 by turning the main switch to **((.))** nothing unusual will happen. No changes are visible in the LCD panel. Indeed, the camera is still set to full program mode. In principle everything functions the same as for the green rectangle setting. I can use the camera in exactly the same way, I only need to make sure that I don't turn the input dial inadvertently. However, it is a different matter if I turn it intentionally to call up some special function or setting.

Shifting the Exposure/Shutter Speed Values

Program mode is only capable of choosing one pair of aperture/shutter speed values on its exposure curve, it is not possible to change this combination (in the no-nonsense program mode) and still allow the same amount of light to expose the film.

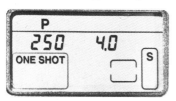

Automatic exposure setting in program mode.

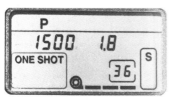

Shift correction in the direction of a faster shutter speed.

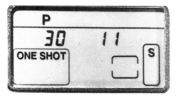

Shift correction in the direction of a slower shutter speed.

Turn the input dial to the right without touching any other buttons and the shutter speed will be increased, simultaneously the aperture will open up. Turn the input dial to the left and the shutter speed will be reduced, simultaneously the aperture will be stopped down.

What happens is that you lightly press the release, the camera takes the appropriate readings and displays the resulting settings in the viewfinder and also in the LCD panel. Now you have 8 seconds within which to effect the shift.

This special function, together with the partial metering function, are the two facilities that I use most often with my EOS 600. Usually I wish to increase the automatically-programmed shutter speed as it is often a little too slow for my liking. On the other hand it is sometimes important to stop down the aperture as much as possible to obtain adequate depth of field.

The shift setting cancels out automatically after the 8 seconds display time has elapsed, both the aperture and shutter speed settings disappear and the exposure mode returns to its predetermined settings. The same happens when an attached flashgun is ready. Shift and flash are incompatible.

This subject is unevenly illuminated. The **P** mode indicated 1/60th at ƒ4; I changed to ƒ2 and a 1/250th.

Above: this subject is shown to good effect by being in focus from front to back. For subjects that extend away from the camera I usually use the shift facility until I find a suitable aperture.

Right: evening scene in Bonn. Flash shot with the EOS set to Av, an exposure compensation of −1.5, and using the EOS 35-105mm, ƒ3.5-4.5.

EXP.COMP – Intentional Over- Or Underexposure

This function allows exposure compensation at half-stop intervals up to 5 *f*-stops.

- Press the EXP.COMP button on the left camera shoulder. **00** ± will appear in the LCD panel. Keep EXP.COMP button pressed and turn the input dial:
- to the right increases the exposure in half stops (compensation = overexposure)
- to the left decreases the exposure in half stops (correction = underexposure)

Display after EXP.Comp button is pressed.

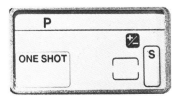

Exposure compensation; underexposure of one *f*-stop has been programmed.

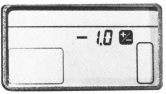

Display for programmed exposure compensation; release has been pressed.

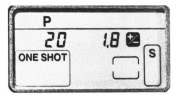

Display for programmed exposure compensation after release has been pressed. The exposure compensation warning ± also appears in the viewfinder.

Left: light from light.
The exposure was determined by spot metering for the horizon in the background but focusing on the glass of the paraffin lamp.

To cancel an exposure compensation:

Press EXP.COMP button and simultaneously turn the input dial in the opposite direction until **0.0** appears again in the LCD panel.

Alternatively, turn the main switch to the green rectangle and the exposure compensation (together with any other special function setting) will be cancelled. Then turn the main switch back to **((.))** or **A**.

Exposure compensation by EXP.COMP button is easier to enter and to cancel than by changing the film speed setting. Moreover, you are reminded of having entered a compensation by the displays, both in the viewfinder and in the LCD panel.

Subjects where Exposure Compensation is Advisable

The following kinds of subjects tend to need compensation by increasing the exposure indicated by the meter from 1 to 2 stops:

- Against the light scenes
- Sunsets
- Small dark subject in front of a large white background
- Snow-covered surfaces

The following subjects may need compensation by reducing the exposure indicated by the meter from 1 to 2 stops:

- Lit streets at night
- Stained glass windows
- Small light subject in front of a large dark background
- Aerial shots

Partial Metering – also with Shift and EXP.COMP

Partial metering, also known as spot metering, means that only a small area at the centre of the frame is metered and not the entire frame. The metering mark is in the circle at the centre of the viewfinder. In this metering mode only about 6.5% of the whole subject area is measured.

Partial metering only makes sense combined with exposure lock. With good reason, exposure lock cannot be de-activated with partial metering, not even if the lens is set to M.Focus or if SERVO has been selected. Partial metering makes exposure compensation virtually redundant because one can measure precisely for the important subject detail which will automatically produce the correct exposure level. Changing over to partial metering from integral metering in either **((.))** or **A** setting is easy. Simply press the partial metering button, situated on the top right of the camera back, after the metering system has been activated by slight pressure on the shutter release. The asterisk beneath the focusing screen will now remind you that partial metering is the selected metering method.

The focus setting by AF mode and the partial metering result is kept locked if:
* *The release is pressed halfway together with pressing the partial metering button, or*
* *As long as the release is kept pressed halfway, the partial metering button can be pressed and released again.*
Partial metering with activated autofocus and lock: select Custom Function Control No.4

I have already stated that it is essential at times, particularly for very contrasty subjects, to separate the exposure lock from the AF function. Let's assume you are studying life through a champagne glass and discover in it the image of a fascinating face. You can measure it from a close range, store the exposure setting and step back to a suitable distance. Now you only need to adjust the focus setting and take the picture.

Keep the metering result in memory by keeping the partial metering button pressed – you press the release half-way first, then press the partial metering button. Now let go of the release button, step back and re-activate the AF mechanism by pressing the release button again. It's simpler than it sounds!

When using flash, the partial metering method will adjust the aperture and shutter speed to the prevailing lighting conditions and generally reduce the exposure settings. The flash exposure itself is not affected by the metering method. Using this metering method it is usually not necessary to effect any cumbersome exposure compensations, which are otherwise often necessary with flash pictures.

Moreover, the partial metering method is also quite suitable for program shift; the mutual adjustment of aperture value and shutter speed that keeps the overall exposure value constant, but adjusts the setting to keep the important value within acceptable range. Naturally, any further exposure compensations will also be considered.

Glykenia, the famous Greek singer. Taken at a performance with T-max 3200 black-and -white film, exposed as ISO 800/30°. I measured the face by partial metering and stored the result by holding the partial metering button.

Av – Aperture Priority Mode: Preselected Aperture with Automatic Shutter Speed Control

You select the aperture – the shutter speed is calculated automatically

Are you familiar with automatic cameras? If the answer is "yes", then you will be quite familiar with the Av program (A = aperture). The first automatic cameras had aperture priority mode, but that was their only "automatic" function. This relatively simple, but highly efficient, aperture priority mode is suitable for a wide range of subjects including:

- If you need to shoot an interior from a tripod with a predetermined completely stopped-down aperture to obtain maximum depth of field.
- If you need to shoot with a predetermined wide-open aperture, to obtain the fastest possible shutter speed under the given lighting conditions, or to pick out a sharply-defined subject against a blurred background.
- To reduce the depth of field by selecting a fully open aperture (selective depth of field)
- If available light and flash illumination need to be carefully balanced.

The above situations present a number of very important arguments in favour of the aperture priority mode that cannot be achieved (or at least, not always) in any other program mode.

One weakness of aperture priority mode needs to be mentioned here – in bright light, when using a fully open aperture, it could easily happen that even the fastest shutter speed is not enough to avoid overexposure, particularly if a fast film is used. In this case **2000** will blink in the viewfinder and the LCD panel.

Av Programming

Switch the EOS on by turning the main switch to **A** or **((.))**. Press the MODE button and simultaneously turn the input dial to the right. **Av** appears in the LCD panel.

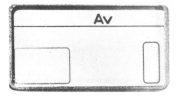

When aperture priority mode is selected.

To change back to **P** either press the MODE button again and turn the input dial until **P** is displayed or turn the main switch to the green rectangle and return it again to the original setting. The latter method is quicker if other special functions are supposed to be cancelled at the same time.

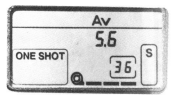

Av and an initial value of ƒ5.6 appear in the LCD panel.

The EOS has been programmed to default to this average value of ƒ5.6 and when you press the release the appropriate shutter speed is also displayed.

The focus lies at the centre of the frame, the aperture fully open, to keep the background unsharp. This setting is best achieved in Av mode.

118

Changing the Aperture Setting

The aperture may be changed in half-stop intervals by turning the input dial. To the left (anti-clockwise) closes the aperture, to the right (clockwise) opens the aperture. The exposure times follow automatically for the given lighting conditions. The whole process is similar to the shift program mode, only the direction in which the input dial has to be turned is different.

In case the light is too bright and 1/2000th sec is still too slow then the number **2000** blinks in the viewfinder and the LCD panel to warn of overexposure. Underexposure is not possible. You will also be warned of danger of camera shake by the audible signal.

Av Partial Metering: with Shift Facility

To change to partial metering when only the area at the centre of the viewfinder is measured, press the partial metering button. Using partial metering in Av mode calls up the same functions as in program mode plus some extra ones. Shift the aperture/shutter speed combination by turning the input dial.

Partial metering on the face of the monkey in Av mode, to be able to choose a wide aperture and thereby the fastest possible shutter speed.

Flash in Av Mode

This program is particularly suited to using flash with available light. The flash is used mainly to fill-in a dark foreground. In this mode you need to watch the shutter speed, as the camera may calculate a rather slow one, but you will be warned of this by the audible signal. If the camera sets a shutter speed slower than 1/8th sec, then everything that is illuminated by the available light will be blurred but the flash-lit foreground will be sharp. The contrast of a sharply outlined main subject against blurred surroundings may be what you want to create.

However, if the intention is to show everything in sharp focus, then you have to:
• Use a tripod if the automatically set shutter speed is too slow, or
• Turn the input dial to select a wider aperture to keep the shutter speed between 1/120th and 1/125th sec.

Unlike the P mode, the shift function will work perfectly in Av mode with flash. In case of danger of overexposure **125** will blink in the LCD panel and the viewfinder. Now it is possible to stop down the aperture unless overexposure is intentional.

Flash-illuminated main subject in sharp focus against a blurred background. Av mode, aperture set to ƒ22, resulting in a shutter speed of 3 seconds, I then released the flash and panned the camera at the same time.

When using flash in Av mode, partial metering of the available light works perfectly well; it is therefore possible to adjust the exposure for a light detail and store it, the release is then triggered which illuminates the foreground by a precisely measured flash.

Proceed as follows: keep shutter release pressed halfway, point camera to bring light detail within the partial metering mark, press the partial metering button and let go, move camera for the desired framing and press the release fully!

Tv – Preselection of Shutter Speed with Automatic Setting of Aperture

You choose the shutter speed – the camera determines the aperture

Shutter speed priority means that the shutter speed is entered manually with the camera calculating and setting the appropriate aperture. This program is particularly useful for the following situations:

- If a particularly fast shutter speed is required. For example: a sequence of shots with a long lens so the shutter speed must not be slower than 1/500th sec to avoid blurring caused by camera shake. For a print film, underexposure of up to one or one and a half f-stops is not exactly ideal but the film will probably be able to accommodate it; in any case it is preferable to blurred pictures.
- If a particularly slow shutter speed is required, perhaps if a movement is to be shown as a more or less blurred outline to enhance the impact of movement.

In certain flash photographs too, preselection of a longer exposure time also makes sense. Weak points of the Tv program: over- or underexposure is likely if you don't watch the displays for the blinking aperture value.

Tv Mode Functions

Switch on the EOS 600 by turning the main switch to **((.))** or **A.** Press the MODE button and turn the input dial one notch to the right. Tv will appear in the LCD panel.

To return the shooting mode to **P**, either press MODE again and turn the input dial back or turn the main switch to the green rectangle.

In Tv mode the initial shutter speed displayed is 1/125th sec. As soon as the release is pressed halfway the appropriate aperture is also displayed in the LCD panel as well as in the viewfinder display. If the aperture value in the viewfinder blinks, over- or underexposure is indicated.

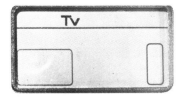

When shutter speed priority mode is selected.

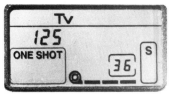

Tv and an initial value of 1/125th appear in the LCD panel.

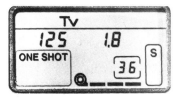

When the release is pressed halfway, the appropriate aperture is also displayed.

Value of largest available aperture blinks: danger of underexposure.
Value of smallest available aperture blinks: danger of overexposure.

As the shutter speed is entered manually and the EOS assumes that the photographer is fully aware of what he is doing, no camera-shake warning is given.

Tv Shift – Changing the Preselected Shutter Speed

Turning the input dial to the right reduces the shutter speed in half-stop intervals, turning it to the left, increases it.
Blinking aperture values indicate, as previously, danger of over- or underexposure. A shift in the shutter speed/aperture value corresponds to the shift in program mode.

Tv Partial Metering

Pressing the partial metering button will now only change the aperture setting (in Av mode, the shutter speed is changed; in P mode, both the shutter speed and aperture are changed). Shifting is also possible, just as in P or Av modes.

Flash in Tv Mode

The fastest shutter speed possible in flash mode is 1/125th sec. In darkness or at dusk the aperture will be wide open. It is possible to photograph subjects at reasonable distances depending on the range of the flash.

For indirect flash, if the largest aperture value blinks in the viewfinder then the background will be more or less dark. On the other hand, you could always increase the shutter speed until the aperture value stops blinking.

If you wish to keep the background dark, apply an exposure correction of −1 to avoid overexposing the foreground.

As for Flash in Av mode, exposure shift and partial metering are fully functional.

Manual Setting of Aperture and Shutter Speed

Manual Program: Useful in a Variety of Situations

When we change over to manual mode, aperture and shutter speed have to be set manually. However, even in manual mode the EOS offers far more than a conventional manual camera. For a start, it keeps you informed of whether the chosen setting corresponds to the correct exposure level. And manual refers only to the setting of aperture and shutter speed, the autofocus function is still fully active unless the lens is switched to M.FOCUS. Moreover, a system flash will provide the correct amount of illumination if the camera is set to manual mode.

The following situations could benefit by using manual mode:
- Several shots to be taken with the same settings. This would be the case for copying, when a variation in reflectance of the items is not supposed to affect the exposure.
- If the settings for each exposure are to be changed quickly and in a certain way.
- Long exposures of any length, particularly more than 30 sec.
- Multiple exposures.
- Trick shots with flash and for accessories not dedicated to the EOS system.

Using Manual Mode

Switch the EOS on by turning the main switch to either **((.))** or **A.** Press the MODE button and simultaneously turn the input dial one notch to the left. **M** and initial values of **125** for the shutter speed and *f*5.6 for the aperture will appear in the LCD panel.

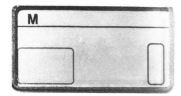

Changing to manual mode; press the mode button and at the same time press the input dial until **M** appears in the LCD panel.

As soon as **M** is selected, nominal values of **125** for the shutter speed and **5.6** for the aperture also appear.

Returning the function setting to **P** is done either by pressing the MODE button and turning the input dial in the opposite direction or by turning the main switch to the green rectangle.

In the viewfinder **M** will appear to remind you that you have to set aperture and shutter speed yourself.

The shutter speed may now be reduced by turning the input dial to the right and increased by turning it to the left.

To change the aperture, press either the manual aperture set button, which is situated at the front of the camera body on the lower left side of the lens bayonet, or the display panel illumination button while simultaneously turning the input dial. Turning it to the right closes the aperture, turning it to the left opens the aperture.

Metering for Correct Exposure in Manual Mode

In the LCD panel the shutter speed value is replaced by the following symbols as soon as either button is pressed; these inform you of how the aperture has to be changed to achieve correct exposure:

OP = open: open up aperture
oo = no correction necessary: correct level set
CL = close: stop down aperture

These abbreviations together with the aperture value also appear in the viewfinder display.

I always set the shutter speed first then adjust the aperture until oo indicates that the exposure is correct. Of course it is possible to take extra shots with a deliberate exposure compensation.

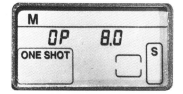

Underexposure: open the aperture.

Overexposure: stop-down the aperture.

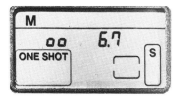

Correct exposure: take the picture.

It is possible to reverse this procedure by selecting Custom Function Control No.5 thereby being able to change the aperture by a simple turn of the input dial and to enter the shutter speed by pressing either button together with the input dial.

M Partial Metering

Naturally, partial metering is also possible in manual mode. Press the partial metering button while pressing the manual aperture set button. A green asterisk will appear in the viewfinder. The shutter speed or aperture that have been entered manually are not changed; however the exposure abbreviations – **OP**, **oo**, and **CL** – do change when the metering mode is switched from integral to partial.

Long Exposures of any Duration

Turning the input dial to the left selects slow shutter speeds (1" = 1 sec). If we continue turning the dial we eventually reach half a minute (30"), turning the dial one more time, the next display is **bulb** (both in the viewfinder and the LCD panel). This description is a left-over from the very early days of photography when the release used to be triggered by a rubber bulb. Today this term has been adopted to indicate a non-automatic long exposure, i.e. the shutter stays open as long as the finger is kept on the release.

Reproduction from a book. If a series of copies have to be made then it is better to set the EOS to manual mode.

The elapsed time appears in the frame counter of the LCD panel; first the seconds from 1 to 30. After the first 30 seconds have elapsed, a black bar appears, and the next 30 seconds are counted down; after one minute a second bar is added, and after one and a half minutes a third. After two minutes have elapsed, the count-down process with the bars is restarted.

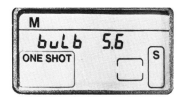

The display for long exposure "bulb".

The aperture may be changed by pressing the manual aperture set button and simultaneously turning the input dial.

For long exposures it is best to use the remote release 60 T3, which can only be attached to the terminal in handgrip GR 20. The release button may be locked in the open position by sliding a switch on the remote release.

The longest exposure time that can be automatically set by the exposure program is 30 seconds. However, there is a trick, the AEB

126

function which will be explained later, that can be used to extend the automatically controlled exposure time. This is done by soft release through the depth of field check button.

When giving long exposures from a tripod the eyepiece has to be covered to prevent stray light from entering the viewfinder and confusing the metering. In the shoulder pad of the carrying strap you will find a small rubber pad which fits over the eyepiece.

Flash in M program – the Creative Flash Mode

If a system flash is attached to the EOS 600 and the camera is set to manual mode, you are free to choose any shutter speed between 1/125th and 30 secs and also bulb. Should you have set a faster shutter speed than 1/125th sec, then the camera will automatically reset it to 1/125th sec as soon as the release is pressed halfway down because the frame would not be completely exposed using a faster shutter speed. The flash output of the system flashgun adjusts automatically for the selected aperture.

Creative possibilities:
• For close-ups in the open, the background can be shown darker if an exposure compensation of –2 is set. To do this, set the shutter speed to 1/30th sec and choose a suitable aperture so as to display **oo** in the viewfinder and LCD panel. Now change the shutter speed back to 1/125th sec and make the exposure. The result will be an underexposed background by two stops. This effect can be increased by presetting the shutter speed to 1/15th or even 1/8th sec. Less severe underexposure would result if the shutter speed was preset to 1/60th sec but don't forget to set it back to 1/125th immediately before making the exposure.
• The EOS is used with a non-system flashgun, or a system-adapted flashgun by another manufacturer (Cullmann, Metz) and used in sensor-mode.
• Long exposure with fill-in flash.
• A dark room is illuminated by several flashguns. Open the shutter of the EOS, supported on a tripod, then trigger the manually released flashguns which are placed around the room at carefully selected positions.

Perfect sharpness from close-up to far away. The depth program calculated the correct aperture and focus setting to place the subject within the depth of field.

Depth of Field

Previewing the Depth of Field by button

The depth of field check button is situated directly above the manual
aperture set button. Pressing this button stops down the aperture to the
selected value. Although the image in the viewfinder gets darker,
usually you can still see how much of the subject depth is shown in
acceptably sharp focus.

This button is also used for a clever trick:

• It will store the AF-controlled location of the depth of field (focus
  setting) and the exposure regardless of whether it was by integral or
  partial metering mode. All you need to do is to press the depth of field
  check button after the lens has been focused and aperture and
  shutter speed determined. You can release both buttons (release and
  partial metering) as long as the depth of field check button is kept
  pressed. The values are retained and shift may be applied to the
  aperture/shutter speed combination by turning the input dial.
• The depth of field check button activates metering of the subject with
  the appropriate viewfinder display and if the partial metering button
  is pressed at the same time then the metering is done in that mode.
• The depth of field check button blocks the release if it is pressed
  before the release is pressed. Now it is possible to press the release
  fully down and start the shutter by releasing the depth of field check
  button. I use this method sometimes with long exposures. Releasing
  a button causes less camera shake then pressing one.

DEPTH – The Depth of Field Mode

If it is important to capture a precisely defined subject depth in sharp
focus, you can measure the closest point to be still sharply depicted and
then the farthest point. The EOS 600 will now automatically select the
correct aperture and focus setting to provide the correct depth of field.

• Press the MODE button and turn the input dial until **DEPTH** appears
  in the LCD panel.
• Point the EOS at a subject detail at the close limit of the subject depth
  and press the release halfway; it can even be pressed fully down, no
  exposure will be made at this point. The audible signal will indicate
  that the lens has focused on this detail and **dEP 1** will be displayed.
• Now focus on a point at the farthest limit of the subject depth that
  needs to be shown in sharp focus, and **dEP 2** will appear as
  confirmation that the lens has focused.

- Select correct framing, press release halfway the third time and keep it pressed. The calculated aperture and shutter speed appear in the LCD panel.
- Check the shutter speed and release if it is satisfactory. If the shutter speed is too slow for hand-held shooting, use a tripod, or move further away from the subject as longer focusing distances result in greater depth of field for the same aperture.

If the light is sufficient and the depth of field required is not excessive then this process is quite quick. In any case, quicker than it sounds!

Part V

Making the Most of EOS 600's Special Features

The topical subject of AF

Autofocus or Manual – either or both: AF + M

EOS lenses feature a manual focusing option once automatic focusing is de-activated using the AF/M.FOCUS switch. However, in my experience I have found that, in most situations, the AF control leads more quickly and precisely to the desired result. Whenever this is not the case I switch it off.

AF control in ONE SHOT setting

ONE SHOT is the term for normal autofocus operation. Focusing is set by holding the release in the half-way position. The normal procedure is as follows:

- Cover the subject with the AF frame in the centre of the viewfinder.
- Activate AF control by pressing the release half-way until correct focusing has been set and stored, notified by the in-focus indicator lighting up in the viewfinder panel and an audible signal.
- Move the camera slightly until the subject is framed as desired in the viewfinder – then press the release fully.

If the exposure has to be specially matched to the final composition. Let go of the release, move the switch on the lens to **M.FOCUS** (AF off) and then press the release fully.

SERVO – Focus and Exposure Tracking

Only when the main switch is set to **((.))** or **A** can this function be activated.

- Press and hold AF mode selector button, situated under the switch cover on the camera back.
- Rotate the input dial in either direction. The LCD panel will alternate between **SERVO** and **ONE SHOT**.

SERVO setting before release is pressed

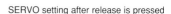

SERVO setting after release is pressed

Focus and exposure input now adjust automatically – practically without delay – to all changes in distance and brightness. There is no shutter release block. It is therefore possible to get unsharp pictures if the focusing process is not completed. In addition, it is vital to get the most important detail of the picture within the AF measuring frame. The sharpest focus is only obtained in the centre. Is there, then, no way of placing the focus away from the centre of the frame using SERVO operation?

It IS possible using a trick explained in the next chapter.

The advantage of SERVO does not lie in the careful composition of pictures. SERVO is used more for snapshots, making it easier to capture more or less fast movements. This is the first EOS to measure the speed of a movement towards, or away from the photographer, which is taken into account when setting the focus. Incidentally, I find it remarkable how many pictures of moving subjects come out sharply focused with the help of the SERVO AF control. For the reason mentioned above – dispensing with memory storage which cannot be reconciled with following a fast moving subject – it cannot be expected that every single snapshot comes out perfectly sharp but with the help of the SERVO AF control the percentage of reject pictures can be considerably reduced.

Please remember: In SERVO setting, there is no audible in-focus signal just the camera-shake warning.

Portrait in a mirror.
The focus was adjusted for the reflection in the mirror. Indirect illumination by halogen light and daylight film (Ektachrome 400) resulted in a warm-coloured rendering.

If the focus is to be set for a particular detail which is not placed at the centre of frame, then it is necessary to set the EOS to AF ONE SHOT mode. The alternative would be to focus manually.

Snappy SERVO operation with Depth of Field Check Button

Now for focus and exposure tracking combined with memory storage.

You have just pressed the release half-way and are panning the EOS 600. The AF control continually adjusts to the new target and the exposure values in the viewfinder will light up. Both may be locked by pressing the depth of field check button. You have then stored both focus and exposure and can alter the framing of the subject. In this way you combine the advantages of SERVO with those of the ONE SHOT operation.

But there is more to come; you can even fix the focus setting and exposure separately, one after the other. Simply press the release halfway, release it again, hold down the depth of field check button and press the release fully home.

Nudes:
Top: nude snapshot.
Bottom: an arranged shot which has been included to illustrate the situation of nude photography rather than as a perfect example.

135

Storing focus and exposure separately:

- *Press release halfway to obtain correct AF focus. Let go of release.*
- *Pan camera. When the subject area desired for exposure adjustment is framed in the viewfinder, press and hold down the depth of field check button.*
- *If necessary, the framing of the subject may be further adjusted. Fully press release.*

Don't content yourself with reading about it – try it out for yourself.

Another possibility: store the exposure, correct the focus setting before actually releasing. Try partial metering. As long as the partial metering button remains pressed, the exposure setting is stored. The AF control is activated on pressing the release. If it is to remain switched off, press the depth of field check button in addition to the partial metering button.

Snapshot. The continuous focus adjustment in SERVO AF mode ensured perfect sharpness for this lively scene.

The Latest Refinement – AF Control with Manual Correction

Each focus setting read by the AF control and stored by pressure on the button can be corrected – especially if we are talking about close objects – flowers, portraits, etc. For instance, we have set the focus automatically on the edge of a flower but wish to have the stamen in focus, which is 1cm further away. So we simply lean forward one cm and bring the focusing plane over the stamen.

Example: a tree behind a gate – the AF control brings the gate post into sharp focus. We switch the lens to M.FOCUS and adjust the focus manually for the branches of the trees. It is best to cradle the lens with the left hand so that the index finger resting on the switch can turn the AF control on and off.

Custom Function Control 7 – manual focus adjustment of ultrasonic lenses after autofocus.

The particularly sophisticated EOS lenses with ultrasonic motor (e.g. EF 50mm, f1; 300mm, f2.8 L; 28-80mm, f2.8-4; all very fast lenses) can be manually adjusted without using the focus mode switch. This requires a basic program change which should preferably be set on the EOS 600 once and for all and left.

Programming the EOS for manual correction after autofocus for ultrasonic lenses

---

- *Hold down black and blue buttons behind the switch cover on the camera back.* **1** *appears in the LCD panel.*
- *Turn input dial to the right until* **7** *appears.*
- *Press partial metering button. Bar symbol confirms the function is activated.*

When it really counts – 5 frames per second

A 36-exposure film in 7.5 seconds

This EOS has the fastest film winder of the series. In **S** setting (= single shot) the rate depends on the photographer's ability to move his finger in a rhythmical sequence. Under favourable conditions this can produce just over two pictures per second. This is adequate for most snapshot situations. It naturally takes longer when the AF control has a lot of ground to cover between each shot; remember: the shutter is released only after the focus has been set.

Switching to **C** (= continuous) increases the rate of shooting quite considerably at up to 5 frames per second.

• Open the switch cover and hold down the blue button. Turn the input dial in either direction until a **C** appears in the LCD panel.

Continuous shooting mode. The shutter will be released as long as the finger is kept on the release button.

If the EOS is set for ONE SHOT each pressure on the release triggers one shot after another – continuously – at the rate of 5 frames per second. If you hold down the release for a good 7 seconds, an entire film is exposed and is then immediately rewound.

C + ONE SHOT – continuous snapshot sequence

The other EOS models manage 3 frames per second. But whether 3 or 5, the high speed allows no continuous focus adjustment between individual shots. The AF control provides the focus setting for the first picture and all other shots trip along behind at the same setting. That means the EOS 600 must focus on an object which does not change its distance from the photographer or not to any significant degree.

There is no doubt that the fast shooting rate of the EOS 600 offers the chance of capturing interesting phases of quick dances or sporting events.

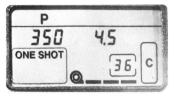

Continuous shooting mode setting: 5 frames per second are possible.

One of a sequence of fast shots.

C + SERVO – somewhat slower but with continuous focus adjustment

If we combine C with SERVO, the AF attempts to take into account all changes in distance which occur between the individual shots (without necessarily succeeding in every single case!). This naturally means that the rate of shooting is reduced. The exposure readings are taken in rapid succession. With wide-angle lenses this still allows shooting rates of between 3 and 4 frames per second, but with longer lenses the rate could be cut to 2 frames per second.

Most pictures will be in sharp focus but not all. Every once in a while the shutter could be released too soon. This operating mode is handy for snapshots at shows, for stage photography, and, not least, for rather more lively portraits.

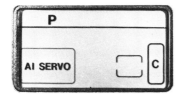

Setting for continuous shooting with focus adjustment between frames

A better chance for short distances – sequence shots with flash

With close subjects at a distance of about 0.7 to 3m (in favourable cases, for instance combined with a particularly fast lens and very high speed film, up to and beyond 5m) as many as 5 flash exposures can be made per second using ONE SHOT + C operation. SERVO + C operation is even more effective as the frequency of shots is thereby reduced to 3 to 4 frames per second. This means a greater safety margin regarding the recharging time of the flash unit. Of course, such fast flash sequences can, in any case, only be achieved with the help of a great reduction in the flash output. On the EOS system flashguns from Canon (Speedlite 300 EZ and 420 EZ) the flash output can be reduced to 1/16th or even 1/32nd of full power when the unit is switched to manual. SCA 300 flashguns by Cullmann or Metz, attached to the EOS by SCA 312 adapter, are switched to **W** (manual operation with reduced output). Of course, in all these cases, there is no automatic exposure metering. The EOS itself should preferably be set to **Av** or **M**. In addition, the widest possible aperture should be set. The guide numbers depending on zoom reflector position lie between:

$f4 - f8$ for ISO 100
$f5.6 - f11$ for ISO 200
$f8 - f16$ for ISO 400
$f11 - f22$ for ISO 800
$f16 - f32$ for ISO 1600
$f22 - f45$ for ISO 3200

You are the Timer

Self-timer with 10 second countdown

The self-timer is used for many reasons, often to include the photographer in a picture. I use this function principally to give long exposures without danger of camera-shake or having to use a cable release. A tripod should be used to support the EOS but a small table or clamp will do just as well.

To set the self-timer; hold down the blue button behind the switch cover and turn the input dial in either direction until the self-timer symbol appears within the rectangle on the right of the LCD panel.

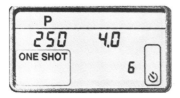

The shutter of the EOS has been released, the 10-second countdown is running. The number next to the box indicates that 6 seconds are left of the sequence.

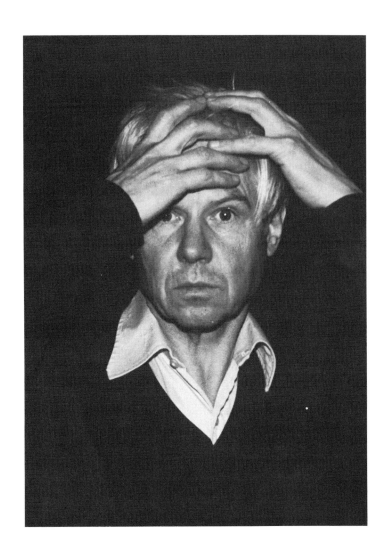

A hair-raising experience it seems – self portrait with self-timer.

The self-timer can be used in AI SERVO or ONE SHOT. To cancel the self-timer function, hold down the blue button again and turn the dial until **S** or **C** appears. Or more simply; quickly turn the main switch to the green rectangle and back again if necessary. This restores all normal functions: **P – ONE SHOT – s**, and cancels all special ones.

When the release is pressed the autofocus is set and stored and the self-timer operation indicator next to the release will begin to blink. The shutter releases automatically 10 seconds after being pressed. Two seconds before shutter release, the indicator starts blinking faster. The countdown sequence is displayed in the LCD panel.

Please note: both the exposure and the AF setting remain locked from the start of the countdown. Nothing can be altered. So if I want to be shown perfectly sharp I have to focus on a substitute object next to which I can position myself before pressing the button. This substitute focusing point will usually be one of the companions with whom I wish to be photographed. In situations like these I usually stick to P mode with the AF function switched off.

To stop the self-timer during countdown; simply press the black button behind the switch cover. You can then either start another sequence or cancel the self-timer function altogether.

Self-timer with Flash

In order to achieve perfect results when using system flash with the self-timer, remember that the flash should already be charged and switched on before the release is pressed. If it is switched on later the picture may still be all right depending on your luck and the state of the battery.

Special cases for self-timer

Self-timing can be combined with most special functions; exposure compensation, three-frame bracketing, multiple exposures, and long exposures.

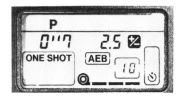

The LCD panel is full of information. Shown here; automatic self-timer and 3-exposure bracketing with exposure compensation.

One release – three pictures

AEB – 3 frame auto exposure bracketing of your choice

In AEB mode, pressing the release once automatically triggers three frames, each with a different exposure.

Setting AEB: hold down the yellow and black buttons beneath the switch cover; **0.0** and **AEB** appear in the LCD panel. Turn the input dial to the desired bracketing value. Depending on what value you set, the range is up to ± 5 stops in 1/2 stop increments, the first shot will be underexposed by that amount, the second shot will be correctly exposed, and the third shot will be overexposed. The focus is set before the first shot and remains stored in memory. Even in SERVO setting there is no adjustment of focus between the individual shots.

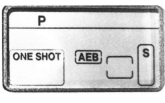

AEB function programmed.

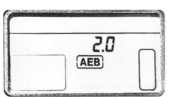

If the yellow and black buttons are pressed simultaneously and the input dial is turned, values appear in the LCD panel which indicate the difference in exposure around the metered exposure level.

With the EOS 620, the AEB function is immediately cancelled once a three-frame bracketing has been fired off. The 600, on the other hand, retains this function until it is manually cancelled. I find that more practical. After all, this special effect is most often used for subjects which may be unique and we only have the chance to photograph them once. A wise man brackets the exposure if there is any doubt, just to make sure.

It isn't every day that I shoot a bracket with an exposure difference of four or five stops – at 4 stops bracketing the overexposed picture receives 512-times as much light as the underexposed one. Usually I bracket by half a stop. If the EOS is loaded with slide film, I quite regularly set an EXP.COMP adjustment of –0.5. As a result I then get a correctly exposed shot (i.e one that is correct according to the camera's exposure control), one which is underexposed by 1/2 a stop, and one which is underexposed by a whole stop.

To cancel the AEB function, hold down the yellow and black buttons again and reset **0.0** by turning the input dial. Or more simply; quickly turn the main switch to the green rectangle and back again if necessary. This restores the normal functions and cancels all special ones.

Another possibility, switch on the Canon EOS system flashgun. As soon as it is ready to flash, the AEB function is cancelled but all other special functions set on the camera are unaffected. If necessary the flash can then be switched off.

Of course, this means that AEB flash photography is impossible. However, SCA 312 RL-adapted flashguns first trigger two flash shots and then cancel the AEB function. I can't vouch for correct exposure in this case.

There again, under certain circumstances I can take AEB flash shots with flashguns which do not conform to the system. This works, for example, using the Leica SCA 351 adapter. A Cullmann or Metz flashgun connected, using this adapter, fires off three flash shots one after another. I naturally have to set the unit to **W** (reduced power). The EOS should preferably be set to manual mode. The AEB exposure factor which has been set cannot, of course, influence the flash exposure in this case – it may, at the most, affect the prevailing light.

Auto Exposure Bracketing in different shooting modes

P mode: aperture and shutter speed change between individual shots.
Tv mode: only the aperture settings change.
Av mode: only the shutter speed changes.
M mode: only the shutter speed changes. The exposure setting can be retained independently of the metering.
DEPTH mode: only the shutter speed changes.

Three frame sequence with bracketing factor of 2. One picture is correctly exposed (centre), the one on the left is underexposed by a factor of 2, the other (right) is overexposed by the same factor.

Special tricks with auto exposure bracketing

As already indicated, the exposure bracketing can also be shifted towards under- or overexposure by the additional setting of exposure compensation. If I use the EXP.COMP button to enter the same factor as for AEB but with a minus sign, then I get two others which are underexposed to different degrees, in addition to my correctly-exposed shot. If I choose the plus-factor, I shift everything towards overexposure. The combination of AEB and multiple exposure is particularly interesting.

All about multiple exposures

ME = Multiple Exposures

The multiple exposure function ME allows several exposures on one frame.

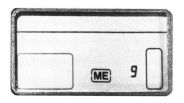

Selection of the number of individual exposures on one frame.

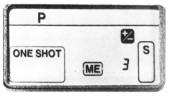

Multiple exposure function programmed. Three further exposures are left. An exposure compensation has been chosen for the sequence.

145

Setting ME: simultaneously press MODE and EXP.COMP buttons on the left shoulder of the camera. ME appears in the LCD panel (and in the viewfinder when the release is pressed half-way). The number 1 beside it can now be changed to a number between 2 and 9 by turning the input dial. You can, then, make up to 9 exposures on one frame. After each individual shot the exposures are counted down on the LCD panel so you always know how many more shots you can expose on this particular frame. This is important because the individual partial exposures may be made at quite long intervals.

To cancel the ME setting: once a multiple exposure has been completed then the ME function is cancelled. To manually cancel, or even interrupt it in the middle, press the same two buttons once more and reset the number to 1. For total deletion together with all other special functions; turn the main switch to the green rectangle.

2 to 9 exposures on one frame

Multiple exposures should also be repeated several times – rather too many than too few. With this type of technique, success cannot be guaranteed every time. Whether or not one superimposes the individual subjects in such a way that the finished picture also looks interesting is not only a matter of creative skill but also of luck.

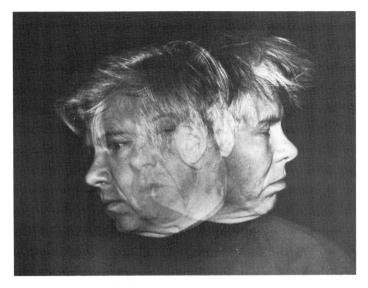

Quite a combination – AEB/ME mode with flash exposure and taken by self-timer!

146

We must differentiate between two very different situations with regard to exposure. Let us assume we are taking three heads, placed in different corners of the frame, lit from the front before a black background or at night. In such a case, the individual images do not overlap, they are arranged next to one another. Each individual subject therefore requires its own full lighting. That means exposure compensations are not required.

If, on the other hand, we are photographing three landscape subjects, each of which fill the whole frame then each individual subject must receive somewhat less exposure. We can only allow it 1/3 of the light which it would normally receive if taken on its own. If, however, we are piling up a larger number of exposures, then it is better to allow each a little more than just the proportional amount. The following table offers a rough guide.

Compensations for Multiple Exposures

Number of exposures	theoretical	practical
2	1	−1
3	−1.5	−1
4	−2	−1.5
5	−2.5	−2
6	−2.5	−2
7	−3	−2.5
8	−3	−2.5
9	−3	−2.5

The above values should serve just as a rough guide and must be adjusted considerably according to the situation.

ME – Special creative effects

For the first attempt it is a good idea to choose details well-lit from the front but with a dark background. Particularly interesting effects are produced if each partial exposure is made in a different colour. Place different coloured filters in front of either the lens or the light source. Flash can also be used for good effects.

If one sticks to a dark background, the combination of AEB and ME (input ME 3) makes it possible to create effects which otherwise are possible only with stroboscopic flash. Three phases of movement are recorded, one directly after another, all on one frame.

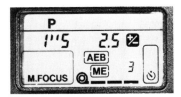

Pressing the release once – 3 exposures on one frame: the combination of AEB with ME, i.e. triple exposure with three shot auto bracketing.

   And if certain conditions are met (see earlier "1 Release – 3 Pictures") then flash can be used – preferably with the help of an extension cable – as sidelight or glancing light. The resulting pictures are then true stroboscopic shots.

One-and-a-half minute fully automatic exposure

We already know how 30 sec can be set as the longest automatically-controlled shutter speed in M or Tv mode. However, we can extend this time limit by setting AEB 0.5 and ME 3 in addition to 30 sec. In manual mode the aperture can be fully opened if required. The system then triggers 2 x 30 sec and 1 x 20 sec (total 1 min. 20 s). In Tv mode a completely dark or black background causes full aperture opening but one of the three half-minute exposures will be made with the aperture closed down by half a stop.

Part VI

EOS Flash Photography

Hints on flash photography with dedicated system flashguns

Hint 1: Secure attachment of flashgun

> *In this section on EOS flash photography the most important flashguns are discussed and, in addition, all the other hints on flash photography which are scattered throughout the book are once more systematically summarized.*

Dedicated system flashguns make flash photography really foolproof. If the flash does not work, the reason could be that the flashgun is not properly mounted in the camera's accessory shoe. Check this by turning the mounting wheel on the foot of the flashgun anti-clockwise. Push the flashgun firmly into the shoe, as far as it will go, and screw the wheel down tightly again.

Hint 2: Flash photography without hesitation

EOS dedicated system flashguns, when connected and charged, set the camera to a shutter speed between 1/125th and 30 sec which is suitable for flash photography. The film speed is automatically taken into account. If we press the release halfway and the flashgun is fully charged a flash-ready symbol appears in the viewfinder. An indicator lights up on the back of the flashgun.

The flash exposure metering is carried out through the lens. Particularly when P mode has been selected we can freely shoot away to our heart's content at everything which is not closer than 0.7m and not further away than – well, how far depends on the film and lens – but the flashgun will illuminate subjects at 5 to 6m even under the most unfavourable conditions.

If Canon flashguns 300 or 420 EZ are attached and ready to flash, distances which cannot be handled by the flash are indicated by signals in the viewfinder when the release is pressed halfway. If the green AF spot blinks the range is too close, if aperture and shutter speed displays blink then the distance is too great. With other makes of flashgun which have been adapted to the system, a green lamp on the back of the flashgun lights up after the shot has been taken to indicate that the subject has been adequately lit.

Colour and black-and-white print films will always be correctly exposed. A compensation may be necessary for slide films.

Hint 3: Very important: exposure compensation of –1 for outdoors and subjects with a dark background

This hint only applies if slide film is used but it is very important. Whenever the background is black, dark or simply at a great distance, the flash-lit foreground will be overexposed. But dark subjects also cause the automatic metering to make the flash give out too much light. In such cases, and that means almost 80% of all flash situations, an exposure correction of –1, or –0.5 at least, must be made or the film speed setting adjusted accordingly. I take almost all flash shots with a correction of this sort. If in doubt, it is better to give the subject too little flash than to swamp it. If we are dealing with a close subject in front of a dark background it is also possible to switch over to partial metering which can make compensation unnecessary.

Exposure compensations for flash photography with slide film

Light subject in front of dark background	–1
Outdoors at night	–1
Indoors with distant background	–1
Dark-toned subject	–0.5
Close subject outdoors in daylight	–0.5 to –1
Very small subject in front of a dark or very distant background	–2

Hint 4: Bounce flash

Indirect lighting is a tried and tested flash method giving good illumination recommended for indoor locations with white walls.

The flashgun's reflector is aimed vertically at the ceiling or at an angle if the subject is further away. This results in a diffuse light source which bathes the subject in a soft light without hard shadows.

Hint 5: Flashed Reflections

The simplest of the numerous interesting methods of illuminating reflections consists of flashing directly into a large mirror with the flashgun mounted on the camera. The light is then reflected from the mirror onto the face of the person seen in the mirror, which is then displayed to the camera, correspondingly well-lit, via the mirror.

This composition was aided by an exposure compensation of –1.

It is hardly the best method for self-portraits. The AF control does, however, allow self-portraits holding the EOS above, or to one side of, the head. The photographer should not be able to see him/herself in the mirror, just the camera and flash.

Hint 6: Make sure the reflector position is adjusted!

The reflectors are adjusted automatically or manually to the focal length of the lens. This makes it possible, on the one hand, to light the whole subject for wide-angle shots and, on the other hand, to achieve a considerable flash range for shots with longer focus lenses or with longer focal length settings.

The combination of a long focal length lens and a wide-angle reflector setting presents no problems for the lighting quality as long as the resulting limitation on flash range is still acceptable. This actually provides particularly even lighting.

The combination of a short focal length lens and the reflector set for lenses with a long focal length must be avoided unless you want a spotlight-type illumination of the centre of the subject field as a special effect.

Hint 7: Take care at short distances

With most flashguns a minimum range of 70cm must be observed. Close-up shots should therefore be taken either with long lenses from a greater distance or by using bounce flash. If necessary, arrange the flashgun at a greater distance from the subject than the camera using an extension cable. Flash ranges of less than 70cm are possible if you switch to M mode.

Flashguns

EOS system flashguns from Canon

Canon supply the following EOS system dedicated flashguns:
- Speedlite 300EZ: compact unit, lightweight and very simple to use. No adjustable reflector.
- Speedlite 420EZ: more powerful but still compact. Reflector angle adjustable through 90°. Features a stroboscope facility.
- Macro Ring Lite ML 3: special macro ring flashgun for automatic exposure at distances of between 2 and 400cm. Only to be used in combination with the macro EF 50mm, $f2.5$ lens.

Swallow at her nest, illuminated by flash.

The 300EZ and 420EZ feature the infrared autofocus control for precise focusing in total darkness. The ring flash has a glowlamp modelling light.

Handling either one of these units couldn't be more simple. Both adjust the reflector automatically to the focal length of lens being used. With the 420EZ the reflector can also be adjusted by hand. Exposure and focus are automatically set by day and night; in the latter case with the AF infrared flash at ranges of between 90cm and 6 or 8m.

> *An extension cable which would make it possible to detach the flashgun from the camera and light the subject from another angle is not yet available.*

Flash photography in the different program modes

Flash photography in P mode

Exposure time: the connected and charged system flashgun automatically sets a shake-free shutter speed of between 1/125th and 1/60th sec.

Aperture and level of exposure: the aperture setting is adjusted to the amount of ambient light in relation to the shutter speed. The amount of light to be delivered by the flash is based on the foreground subject on which the lens is focused.

If there is sufficient light, ambient brightness and flash lighting are combined. In dark interiors and at night, flash lighting takes precedence. Distant backgrounds remain dark. The aperture setting then depends on the subject range – the shorter it is, the more the aperture is stopped down. Partial metering (with main switch at **((.))** or **A**) is possible but shifting of shutter speed and aperture value is not.

Exposure error warning when the release is pressed halfway: shutter speed and aperture values blink in the viewfinder – subject is too far away, move closer and try again.

Only the aperture value blinks: ambient light causes overexposure of the background. A shaded subject in the foreground will nevertheless be correctly lit by the flash.

Flash photography in PIC 1-7

Shutter speed is between 1/125th and 1/60th sec. Aperture and illumination level is adjusted to ambient light with preference given to wide apertures even for close-up shots. This mode allows even weak ambient light to be taken into account in the composition. Exposure error warning with release pressed halfway.

Flash photography in Av mode

Shutter speed: once the aperture has been preset, this is set automatically in the range between 1/125th and 30 sec. In darkness, quite slow shutter speeds may result.

Aperture and illumination level: the aperture setting is preset by hand and the amount of flash required is determined accordingly. The choice of Av flash proves useful when one intends to use small apertures giving greater depth of field.

Exposure error warning when release is pressed halfway. Shutter speed and aperture values blink in the viewfinder. Distance from subject is too great. **125** display (1/125th sec) blinks: subject surroundings will be overexposed, foreground in shadow. Subject correctly illuminated, **30"** (half minute) blinks: main subject will be correctly exposed, background will be dark despite slow shutter speed.

Please note: There is no camera-shake warning when using flash. If a subject in the foreground is shown in sharp focus, the background may be slightly blurred. Hand-held shots are possible up to about 1/8th sec. Attractive contrasts between sharp- and soft-focus can be achieved by the combination of flash and long exposure times of 1/4 sec.

> *When using Av flash mode, apertures of more than f4 should be avoided otherwise exposure errors may occur.*

Flash photography in Tv mode

Shutter speed is set manually, between 1/125th and 30 secs.

Aperture and level of exposure: The aperture setting and flash intensity are automatically adjusted to the shutter speed setting. Large apertures are preferred in darkness.

Exposure error warning with release pressed halfway: shutter speed and aperture values blink in the viewfinder: distance from subject is too great. Maximum aperture value blinks: background will be underexposed because ambient light is too weak to be taken into account. Minimum aperture value blinks: background will be overexposed but the subject will be correctly exposed.

Nudes through unsharply defined framing. Focusing was done through the bent arms or over the heads of other photographers. Illumination was provided by two halogen lights. The pictures top and bottom left were taken with daylight film, the picture at the bottom right was taken on Ektachrome 160 tungsten film.

Flash photography in M mode

Shutter speed is manually set at between 1/125th and 30 sec.

Aperture and level of illumination: the aperture is also set by hand, the flash intensity is automatically controlled for different distances so that the main subject in the foreground is always correctly exposed.

M mode makes correct automatic exposure possible even at close range. With the Canon 420EZ, for example, a subject somewhere at a range between 50cm and – depending on film speed – 1 to 6m will be correctly exposed automatically with an aperture of ƒ22. The distance range appears on the flashgun's LCD panel when the release is pressed halfway.

Exposure error warning on pressing release half-way. The automatic range display appears in the LCD panel. If this blinks, the aperture setting must be changed.

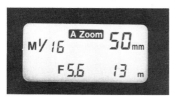

Display of distance range in the flash LCD panel for EOS M-program and entry of aperture ƒ22 at film speed of ISO 100/21°.

Guide numbers for manual flash photography (ISO 100/21°)			
Canon 420EZ Reflector	normal	1/16 output	1/32 output
50mm	35	8.8	6.2
80mm	42	10.5	7.4

In fully manual operation the flashgun is also switched to M and the aperture must be set by hand. If no display is available use the guide number. This, divided by the distance in m, gives the aperture to be set, and when divided by the aperture which has been set, gives the flash range in metres which must not be exceeded. Guide numbers, unless expressly marked otherwise, refer to ISO 100/21° films. In order to determine the guide numbers for a film of twice the speed, they must be multiplied by 1.4, or by 2, for a film of four times the speed.

Framed by the door. One light from the direction of the camera used as a bounced front light and reflected by a projection screen; the other is used from outside the room as indirect sidelight, entering through the half open door.

157

> *When using automatic M flash mode you should never use larger apertures than f4 otherwise exposure errors may occur. Any aperture can be used when it is set by hand if the flashgun is also switched to M.*

Flash photography in DEPTH mode

When flash is used, depth of field mode automatically switches to program mode.

Special flash situations

Flash photography in complete darkness

If the background is to be kept dark – at night, dusk or dawn, in large rooms or outdoors (close subjects in front of distant backgrounds), select P , or Tv or M at 1/125th sec.

If you don't want highlights and side-lighting drowned in a powerful flash, set P 1 or Av (or if you don't mind the background being out of focus, Tv at 1/8th to 1/30th sec). In all these cases, as a general rule, one should make an exposure compensation of one stop (EXP.COMP. –1 or double the ISO rating) or switch to partial metering.

The darker it is, the more difficult automatic or manual focusing becomes. The infrared AF control, coupled with the flashgun, brings everything into focus at ranges between 90cm and 6 to 8m, as well as being correctly exposed.

The infrared AF control can also be used for long exposures without flash: activate AF function by pressing release halfway while the flash is switched on, then switch the flash off.

Using flash in daylight

P is suitable, as well as P 1 (particularly where weak side-lighting should not be overpowered by the flash), or Tv at 1/125th sec. Even in daylight, a compensation of –1 is often, or usually, to be recommended. For flash close-ups with additional daylight or early evening atmosphere I like to use Av at f16 or f22.

Rapid flash sequences

For trick and special effect pictures it is sometimes necessary to fire off quick bursts of flash, one after another. That is only possible with fresh batteries or freshly-charged rechargeable batteries. In addition, we have to reduce the intensity of the flash – so set the flash to M 1/8th, M 1/16th or M 1/32nd (reduced output power settings). The less light the flashgun throws out, the quicker it is recharged. And even if you choose a reasonably fast film only subjects at close range can be lit.

Generally speaking, rapid shots can be taken in all modes. Av and M, however, are particularly suitable. Because it's a question of calculating the aperture according to the distance of the subject and setting it by hand. The 420EZ shows the maximum flash range for the respective aperture setting. The selected aperture of the EOS is even displayed automatically on the flashgun's LCD panel.

And now to the possibilities for rapid shooting:

- With the EOS 600 on C setting an incredible 5 frames per second can actually be taken using flash; the flashgun can manage that provided the batteries are really fresh. A power pack provides an adequate reserve of power in a case like this.
- Automatically triggered three-frame bracketing (AEB).
- 3-frame stroboscope effect shots showing three phases of a moving sequence are also created under the conditions just mentioned if, in addition to the AEB function, ME 3 (multiple exposure x 3) is switched on.
- True stroboscope shots can be achieved with the Canon 420EZ. The unit should be switched to MULTI and set at reduced intensity between M 1/8th and M 1/32nd. The correct flash range for the aperture setting is also displayed in the flashgun LCD panel. As the flash rate is slower – 1 flash per second – M 1/8th or 1/4 makes it possible to photograph subjects somewhat further away. The number of automatically-triggered flashes depends on the shutter speed which is set. The minimum is one second. One flash per second is triggered, plus another one in addition. Strobe flash shots have to be taken from a tripod against a dark background. Using sidelight or glancing light is particularly effective.

The two stroboscopic methods described above are somewhat different. The three-shot method produces a quick succession of shots – the whole sequence within half a second. Moreover, the shutter opens and closes between each shot. The stroboscopic shots with the 420EZ are four times as slow – 2 seconds for 3 flashes and the shutter stays open all the time.

Flash with non-Canon flashguns

> *Warning:* do not use multi-flash adaptors or cable connectors to attach non-EOS flashguns to your camera. Circuits could be blown. Use a slave-cell instead.

Part VII

EOS System Lenses and their Characteristics

The Right Choice

Lenses of Fixed Focal Length

At the moment one can assume that Canon are going to cover the gaps that are left in the limited range of fixed focal length lenses currently offered. In the wide-angle range, the EOS zoom lenses extend down to 20mm but the only fixed focal length under 24mm is a fish-eye. At the other end of the range, the practical limits of tele zooms lie at around the 300mm mark, and they are not usually as fast as fixed focal length lenses, which also have the advantage of being usable with converters.

Zoom Lenses – Lenses with Variable Focal Length

These tend to be better, the shorter the range in focal length. The purchase of a 2x zoom – (a zoom where the longest focal length divided by the shortest equals 2) represents no risk. However, the EOS system offers 3x zooms with excellent reproduction qualities.

I must admit that I am extremely satisfied with the two EF zooms 35-70mm, f3.5-4.5 (rotary zoom) and the 35-105mm (slide zoom). Although I have a healthy scepticism towards zoom lenses, I took most of my holiday pictures (many of the illustrations in this book) with these lenses. My reasons were:

- The most important, most commonly required focal lengths are accommodated in a compact, relatively light unit.
- A simple movement changes the focal length, making constant changing of lenses unnecessary. If you are in a hurry, it is difficult to handle everything at once.
- Close-ups are possible with flash and without any additional accessory.
- Zoom lenses allow a range of special effect and trick shots.
- These two lenses – and this was the decisive factor in my considerations – supply excellently sharp and brilliant pictures.
- The focus can be set very precisely by the following trick; choose the longest focal length setting on the lens, allow the autofocus to set the focus, keep release pressed halfway, change the focal length setting back to the required framing, and release fully.

I find it difficult to be enthusiastic about longer focal length zoom lenses. The lenses offered for the EOS up to focal lengths of 100mm are generally of very good quality. However, in the longer ranges the drop

Fixed focal length AF lenses for the EOS by Canon

Lens	Angle of view	closest focus/cm	max. ratio	min. aperture	filter size
EF15mm f2.4 (Fisheye)	180°	20	1:7.1	22	*
EF24mm f2.8	83°	20	1:7	22	58
EF28mm f2.8	75°	30	1:7.7	22	52
EF50mm U f1 L	46°	60	1:9	16	72
EF50mm f1.8	46°	45	1:6.6	22	52
EF50mm f2.5 (Compact Macro)	46°	5	1:2	32	52
EF85mm U f1.2 L	28°30'	95	1:7.5	16	72
EF135mm f2.8 (Softfocus)	18°	130	1:8	32	52
EF200mm U f1.8 L	12°	250	1:12	22	48
EF300mm U f2.8 L	8°15'	300	1:9	32	48
EF600mm U f4 L	4°	600	1:10	32	48

Autofocus zoom lenses for the EOS by Canon

EF Lens mm	Angle of view	closest focus/cm	max. ratio	min. aperture	filter size
20-35 f2.8 L	94-63°	50	1:6	22	72
28-70 f3.5-4.5	75-34°	39	1:4.5	22-29	52
28-80 U f2.8-4 L	75-30°	50	1:5	22-32	72
35-70 f3.5-4.5	63-34°	39	1:5	22-29	52
35-105 f3.5-4.5	63-23°	86	1:6	22-29	58
35-135 f3.5-4.5	63-18°	95	1:6	22-29	58
50-200 f3.5-4.5	46-14°	120	1:4.5	32	58
50-200 f3.5-4.5 L	46-14°	120	1:4.5	32	58
70-210 f4	34-11°	120	1:4.1	32	58
80-200 f2.8 L	30-12°	180	1:6	32	70
100-200 f4.5 A	24-12°	190	1:7	32	58
100-300 f5.6	24-8°15'	1500	1:3.85	32	58
100-300 f5.6 L	24-8°15'	1500	1:3.85	22	58

* – the Fisheye lens has built-in filters
Lenses with an L in their model description are extremely high quality.
Lenses with U in their model description have an ultrasonic motor which is particularly fast and hardly audible.

in quality is quite noticeable. Longer zoom lenses need a larger number of elements which makes them more liable to stray light than fixed focal length lenses. Zoomed shots therefore lack the brilliance of which a fixed focal length lens is capable.

The various zoom lenses offered are either of the rotating or sliding type.

Rotating zoom: the focal length setting is chosen by turning a ring on the lens tube. This is slower but generally better for shorter focal length ranges. With a slide mechanism the rather short range would be traversed too quickly and could not be controlled as easily.

Slide zoom: the focal length is traversed by sliding a sleeve along the lens tube. This is more suitable for bridging longer focal length ranges, which is generally the case with telephoto zooms.

Extenders for Greater Reproduction Scale

The optical units that are inserted between the camera body and a lens, are used to extend the focal length of that lens on the one hand, and on the other, to reach further into the macro range. To use one of these extenders (or converters) makes sense only if they are offered not just for the far range but also for close-ups (macro lenses). The description of a converter usually includes the factor by which the focal length is increased.

Extender (Converter) Extension Factors		
Factor	*1.4x*	*2x*
Focal length combination		
with 200mm lens	*280mm*	*400mm*
Reproduction scale:		
linear magnification	*1.4x*	*2x*
area magnification	*2x*	*4x*
Loss in lens speed	*1 stop*	*2 stops*

Hint 1: Short Focal Length – Maximum Sharpness from Close-up to Infinity

It is not always desirable to have maximum sharpness from close-up to infinity. However, if it is, then you have to follow these rules:

The smaller the aperture, the greater the focusing distance and the shorter the lens focal length, the larger the depth of field.

A typical wide-angle shot. It required only a moderately stopped-down aperture to bring the whole subject depth into sharp focus.

The depth of field usually extends twice as far behind the focusing plane as in front. For this reason it is best to place the focusing plane in the first third of the total subject depth. If you are using the DEPTH mode this will be done automatically.

The situation is somewhat different in the close range. The depth of field extends equally as much in front of the focusing plane as behind.

Focal Lengths of Lens:

Super wide-angle	15-24mm (very short)	Shows a very large section of the subject at an extremely small reproduction scale
Wide-angle	28-35mm (short)	Shows a lot of the subject at a small reproduction scale
Standard lens	40-55mm	average reduction in scale
Medium telephoto (portrait lens)	70-120mm (long)	reduction in scale is not very pronounced
Long telephoto	135-1000mm (very long)	a small amount of the subject is shown at a relatively large scale

---

Hint 2: Long focal Lengths – Image Creation with Excellent Main Subject Sharpness

A small detail, depicted pin-sharp against a background that is an unrecognizable swirl of colours and shapes – compositions of this type can be most effective. Even the foreground may be unsharp and may partially cover the main subject. The sharper the main subject is against the unsharp back- and fore-ground, the more our attention is drawn to this part of the composition. The important criteria for shots of this nature is not the "depth" of field but the "shallowness" of field. This is achieved by moving close to the subject, using a wide aperture and a long focal length. The AF mode of the EOS is capable of slicing a very thin focused plane out of the subject space.

Hint 3: Space Compressors and Extenders

Wide-angle lenses used close up extend the relative distances into the subject space, a 24mm lens seems to introduce large spaces, pushing everything into the background. Long lenses at large distances, on the other hand, foreshorten distances between the objects, bunching them together. Telephoto shots always look rather two-dimensional. A tree in the foreground with a mountain in the background taken with a 24mm lens near to, will look as if there is 100m distance between the two objects, in the long distance 240mm telephoto shot the same distance seems to have shrunk to a mere 10m.

Hint 4: Dynamic Shapes

Beautiful dynamic shapes of boats, technical equipment, buildings, can be optically enhanced by short focal lengths taken from a low angle at close range. Façades of buildings, towers, cranes – all these are subjects which can be rendered dramatically in this way – provided the camera is pointed at a steep angle.

Hint 5: Grotesque Distortions

The above mentioned recipe for dynamic shapes applied to portraits can produce the most grotesque caricatures. Perhaps you wish to do just that? In this case use the EF 24mm, $f2.8$ wide-angle lens and move to within 30cm of your victim's head. Take the shot at an oblique angle from the top. The head will take on the proportions of a pear with the mouth, further away, quite small. Or perhaps you favour a view from below? The chin will loom over you, disproportionately large. The surreal effects of this can be further enhanced by suitable lighting; direct light from a steep angle from below. You can be sure that your set of pictures will find a place of honour in any rogues gallery.

Hint 6: Close-ups with A Large Proportion of Recognizable Background

Close-ups are usually taken with a moderate telephoto lens for a variety of reasons. If the subject is a butterfly, dragonfly or a beetle, then we are practically forced to use a longer focal length lens. Small, shy creatures cannot be approached too closely. However, if we are interested in flowers, or other small objects that don't run away, and we need to show the background if not pin-sharp, at least reasonably sharp, then we are better served with a short focus lens. The 24mm wide-angle lens has a close-up focusing distance of 20cm. Using a close-up lens this distance can be further reduced without running into complications with the AF or exposure systems of the EOS. A close-up lens reduces the shooting distance and increases the possible reproduction scale.

Façade of a house taken with a 24mm wide-angle lens.

Hint 7: Normal Perspective

For natural-looking perspective the viewing distance for a print can be calculated from the formula – viewing distance = focal length of camera lens x magnification used in making the print. In the case of a projected slide the viewing distance for natural perspective is, focal length of camera lens x magnification used in projection. At the right distance a photograph can have a realism that is absent at other distances.

Hint 8: Good Illumination of Large Interiors

Did you know that the intensity of light from a light source decreases as the square of the distance from the light source? This may sound confusing; what it means is that the intensity of the light of a flash at 2m distance is only one quarter as strong as at 1m distance. The following table demonstrates the relationship more clearly:

Distance: light source to object	% Ilumination intensity
1m	100%
2m	25%
3m	11.1%
4m	6.25%
5m	4%
6m	2.77%
7m	2.04%
8m	1.56%
9m	1.23%
10m	1%

The above table makes an interesting observation which is of great importance to photographic lighting techniques. The intensity of light declines steeply with increasing distance.

Practical conclusion: if we wish to illuminate a certain space uniformly then we have to use a so-called tele-light, i.e. the light source has to be as far from the subject as possible.

Furthermore you should consider that the tele-light will cause reflections from the surfaces in the room, which bounce the light into dark areas and brighten them. This effect can be increased by setting the flash reflector to the wide-angle position. Bounce flash supplies almost ideal, uniform lighting in interiors.

Hint 9: Intimate and distant pictures

I have included hints on lenses to demonstrate the enormous effect that the different focal lengths have on image creation. The way the different focal lengths are used to show the relationship of the person to the fore- and background is most important for the psychological impression we are creating.

- Long focal length lenses – large distance to the foreground; the background has moved away into the distance, the person(s) seem to have moved into the background, they belong to it, appear to be pushed into it.
- Shorter focal length lenses – short distance to the foreground: the background seems to have moved far away, the person(s) dragged right into the foreground, separated from the background.
- Conclusion: if we photograph people at some distance with a long lens their presence does not seem imminent, they are distanced from us.

A portrait, taken with the EF35-105mm ƒ3.5-4.5, zoom set to 100mm.

Part VIII
Special Accessories for the EOS 600

Various Front Lens Attachments

Rubber Lens Hoods

The compact macro EF 50mm, *f*2.5 and the EF 300mm, *f*2.8 have one thing in common; they have an integrated hood. For all other lenses I would recommend that you buy a rubber hood. These are available for narrow and wide-angle lenses (B + W, Hama, Kaiser, Rowi). A further advantage is that they offer some protection to the front of the lens in case you inadvertently knock into something.

Filters and Extension Tubes

What filters are really needed?
For colour slides:
- Colourless UV filter as protection from dust and rain.
- Brown-orange filter R (or KR) 12 for colour-correct pictures when using tungsten slide film in daylight.

For colour print film:
- Colourless UV filter, no other filters are required.

For black and white material:
- Colourless UV filter to protect lens.
- Deep red filter for dramatic skies. The blue of the sky and sea turns nearly black.
- Normal red filter to be used when the deep red filter absorbs too much light.
- Deep green filter for landscapes, to brighten up the green of foliage.

Black-and-white infrared film makes the green of plants appear white while the blue sky and sea appears black. Ektachrome infrared film combined with certain filters produces very interesting colour effects.

Some Comments regarding the Polarising Filter

This is the filter that I use most regularly combined with slide film.

It helps to keep the sky dark blue even in bright sunshine when the sun is at right-angles to the shooting direction.

Shots taken on overcast and wet days also benefit by the use of this filter, the reflected light from wet surfaces is reduced, increasing the intensity of the colours. I would recommend that you try this out yourself.

- Use the more expensive circular polarising filter and your EOS will reward you by assigning the correct exposure which cannot be guaranteed with the cheaper linear polarising filter.
- The position of the filter – it may be rotated in its frame. Turn it and observe the effect in the viewfinder. Some front elements rotate during focusing and you therefore have to adjust the polarising filter after the lens has been focused.
- If you turn the EOS from landscape to upright format, or the other way round, then the filter also has to be adjusted.

Close-up Lenses

Close-up lenses are supplementary lenses. They may not be ideal for copying, where the entire frame right to the edge has to be sharp, because the quality declines towards the edge of the picture. On the other hand, if these attachments are used for close-ups of flowers or small creatures where the main subject is always placed at the centre of the frame, and only incidental items are at the edge, then they offer a useful way of getting close to the actual macro range, particularly if the lens is stopped down to $f5.6$ or smaller. A further advantage; the use of close-up lenses does not reduce the lens speed.

An Interesting Back for the EOS

Integrated clock: Quartz Data Back E 180

To change the standard back for a data back open the camera and push down the locking mechanism on the top of the hinge with your fingernail and bring the back round at an angle then lift it out of the lower hinge. Insert the data back in the lower hinge, push down locking lever with fingernail and align data back with top hinge releasing the locking lever to engage it.

Once fitted, a data back can stay on the camera. Nothing can happen if it is set to **OFF**. The advantage is that you have a clock in the camera and it is possible to check the time without exposing it on film.

The display is either in minutes, hours and the day, or date, month, year. The calendar is programmed to the year 2029. It requires a 3V lithium battery that should last for 3 years. The battery compartment is inside on the right. Shortly before the battery is totally exhausted the word "battery" appears on the LCD panel of the data back to warn you.

This is how you program the E 180

Four buttons are used for the programming of data. These are so thin and lie so deep that you could quite easily break a fingernail trying to get at them. This is intentional to avoid inadvertent use.
* Press the button on the extreme left, this calls up the various functions: date, time, fixed number, consecutive number.
* The second button activates individual numbers in groups of two and any change of entry.
* The third button continues, step by step, the initiated change.
* The fourth button on the extreme right resets the entries to **00**. If **OFF** is set and this button is pressed, the date when the present film was loaded appears in the LCD panel.

Please note: the data to be exposed in the lower right-hand corner of the negative will also be shown in the LCD panel. The exposure of a set of data is confirmed by a thick black bar above the last two groups of numbers in the display.

More Accessories

Eye-sight Correction lenses

Canon offer a variety of these lenses which are available from +3 to –4 dioptres.

Focusing Screens

There are seven types of screens with different focusing aids that you could use with your EOS 600. Each screen comes with its own little tool which facilitates replacement.

For special tasks the following are of interest:
* Type D full matt laser screen with grid. This is useful for the exact alignment of the camera for architectural shots and copying.
* Type H, full matte screen with vertical and horizontal scales in mm for close-up and magnification shots, where the subject has to be shown to a certain scale. Also useful for measuring architectural structures.

And Last but not Least

You will need a bag for your EOS. The camera has to be protected against knocks and against direct contact with water.

Also there are replacement handgrips. The handgrip supplied with the camera is a GR30. It may seem an unnecessary expense, but I would recommend you buy handgrip GR20 with remote control socket together with remote release 60 TL 3. You will not regret this investment. I use the remote release every time the camera goes on the tripod, for close-ups and also for portraits.

Handgrip GR10, the handgrip for the giant with large hands, has no remote release terminal.

Notes